SCHOOL STRESS AND ANXIETY

SCHOOL STRESS AND ANXIETY
Theory, Research, and Intervention

Beeman N. Phillips, Ed.D.
The University of Texas at Austin

HUMAN SCIENCES PRESS
72 Fifth Avenue   3 Henrietta Street
NEW YORK, NY 10011 ● LONDON, WC2E 8LU

Printed in the United States of America
9   98765432

Library of Congress Cataloging in Publication Data
Phillips, Beeman N
     School stress and anxiety.

     Bibliography: p. 153
     1. Personnel service in education.
2. School environment. 3. Child psychology.
4. Anxiety (child psychology) I. Title.
LB1027.5.P525   370.15'3 LC 77-21658
ISBN: 0-87705-324-3

CONTENTS

Acknowledgements   6

Introduction   7

1. Theory and Measurement of School Anxiety   9

2. The Nature of School Stress   32

3. Anxiety in the Elementary School   59

4. Special Studies of Effects of Schooling on
   Anxiety   89

5. Stress, Anxiety, and School Intervention   124

References   153

5

ACKNOWLEDGEMENTS

A number of student-colleagues participated directly in the series of studies and reports that provide the foundation for this book, and I am especially grateful to Russell Adams, Shyam Ahuja, Gail Chandler, Ed Gotts, Charles Harris, Roy Martin, Keith McNeil, Joel Meyers, Piara Pannu and JoAnne Schilhab. I also am indebted to Lorrie Hubbard who aided the project in so many ways and typed the manuscript. It was a privilege to work with all of them.

INTRODUCTION

This book is concerned with an important general problem: the impact of the school environment on children. It
is no exaggeration to say that the schools are seen by many
Americans, including psychologists and educators, as the
means by which pressing social problems will ultimately be
solved. The unemployment problem, the urban and racial
crisis, the loss of guiding values—these and many other
problems are viewed by observers as basically educational
problems. Yet with all of this concern and commitment to
education, the effects of schooling are still a subject of
debate and conjecture. For example, Stephens (1967) re-
minds us that more than half a century of planned manipulations of schooling has produced inconclusive results.

Although the contents concern the effect of the elementary school on children, the major focus of the book is
on the concepts of *stress* and *anxiety*. The original impetus
for this interest was the awareness that the school was ex-
plicitly or implicitly credited with a highly significant impact on the socioemotional life of children. Coupled to this
was the knowledge that the Zeitgeist in American society

was demanding greater achievement by children, more attention to the plight of minority children in many schools, and more emphasis on affective education. In spite of these developments, it had become commonplace in the 1960s to speak out on the need for "schools without failure," and psychologists and educators alike became increasingly concerned about the stresses and anxieties experienced by children in school.

The initial project's purpose, which was supported by a USOE grant to the author, was to analyze antecedents and consequences of anxiety in elementary school children. After this initial formulation, the problem was extrapolated and developed along still other lines. The generally stressful nature of schooling was examined, along with explorations of the nature of adaptive-maladaptive school behavior. We try to show repeatedly the relevance of school stress and anxiety to wide-ranging aspects of child behavior in school. From the breadth of the phenomena in which school stress and anxiety appear as a source of individual differences, the forms of stress and anxiety intervention needed in schools are then delineated, described, and evaluated. In summary, the studies reported had several objectives, but their ultimate emphasis was always the relation of school stress and anxiety to adaptive-maladaptive school behavior. The rest of this book is devoted to these multiple aims, and the many results, issues, and problems, and speculations that emerged in the studies included.

Chapter 1

THEORY AND MEASUREMENT OF
SCHOOL ANXIETY

This chapter proposes that "school anxiety" is a psychologic construct that is relevant to understanding a wide range of individual differences among school children. Before introducing this new construct, however, a more perennial construct—i.e., anxiety—is examined. This provides a foundation for the subsequent explication and interpretation of findings regarding school anxiety. Thus, the chapter does point toward a new construct, but integrates it into an already existing body of psychologic knowledge regarding the effects of anxiety upon human behavior.

DIVERSITY OF VIEWS OF ANXIETY[1]

The term "anxiety" did not gain currency in the psychologic literature until the 1930s (Sarbin, 1968), and professional interest spiraled upward after the publication of Freud's *The Problem of Anxiety* (1936). The extent of this interest is indicated by the rate of publication, which, for the period from 1950 to 1965, averaged more than 200 books, articles, and reports related to anxiety per year

(Spielberger, 1966). Obviously, attention to anxiety is still widespread, not only among psychologists, but also among educators and other professional people, and lay people in general.

In spite of this tremendous interest and productivity, a comprehensive and widely held theory of anxiety has failed to emerge. One reason is that "anxiety as a hypothetical construct has been defined operationally with reference to many diverse criteria" (Chandler, 1969). This is revealed in the views expressed in the contributions to *Anxiety and Behavior* (Spielberger, Ed., 1966), the diversity of which is represented by the following excerpts:

a. Cattell (1966) states that ". . . anxiety arises from a threatened deprivation of an anticipated satisfaction when the threat does not carry complete cognitive certainty [p. 47]." But he goes on to point out that anxiety is only generically similar to fear, and that uncertainty stems from (a) uncertainty of rewarding mechanisms in the objective world, (b) uncertainty of the individual's own impulses, and (c) the individual's cognitive difficulty in appraising them (i.e., the uncertainties referred to).

b. Izard and Tomkins (1966) state that anxiety is a negative affect. They postulate eight innate affects, and subsume anxiety under the affect "fear-terror." They further use anxiety and fear interchangeably on the conviction that there are no useful theoretic distinctions between them.[2] In addition, fear usually occurs in conjunction with other affects (thus, other affects frequently can be considered as concomitants of fear, i.e., anxiety). Especially significant is the combination of fear-terror and interest-excitement, since where there is an oscillation between anxiety and excitement, with anxiety leading to avoidance and excitement leading to creativity, the ambiguity can be resolved toward effective, creative functioning [pp. 122–123]. Finally, they consider the affect system as the primary motivational system.

c. S. B. Sarason (1966) states that ". . . we take seriously the implications of the possibility that high anxiety scores (using questionnaire or self-report measures), except perhaps in a small number of instances, do not reflect what may be termed unambiguous anxiety or even some attenuated manifestation of it, . . ." and that ". . . a high anxiety score may be tapping not anxiety but coping tendencies [p. 74]." Later, he says: "I have no doubt that in the early years of life unambiguous anxiety is a frequent and highly upsetting experience. As the child grows older, however, such experiences become increasingly infrequent as a result of the different ways a child has of coping with anxiety. It is not only that a child defends against anxiety (in the psychoanalytic sense of that word) but also that the consequences of such defense lead to cognitive processes and . . . interrelationships which vary widely in *their* consequences [p. 77]."

d. Grinker (1966) relates anxiety to the stress response, which is measured psychosomatically. He also states that there is very little "free anxiety." Instead, individuals tend only to be anxiety prone, and one must manufacture anxiety by finding out what an individual is susceptible to. In this connection, he reports that blocking interpersonal communication is one of the best, most reliable ways to arouse anxiety. In conceptualizing phases of anxiety, in order of increasing severity or intensity, he identifies the following levels: alertness, apprehension, free anxiety, and panic (with the anxiety-prone individual, who has been anxious, being at the second level). He further stresses that personality is important to the stress response (e.g., a person's emotional stability), and that the anxiety response is not simply the inverse of defense.

e Malmo (1966) conceptualizes anxiety in terms of the clinical type of anxiety (i.e., as pathologic anxiety), and utilizes the activation concept. In pathologic anxiety there is a deficiency in homeostatic mechanisms, e.g., the failure of normal habituation of blood pressure reaction in response to *repeated* stresses. This lack of habituation leads to physiologic overreaction to stress and related consequent losses in behavioral efficiency.

f. Wolpe (1966) takes the position that ". . . neurotic anxiety is nothing but a conditioned emotional habit . . . [which involves] a sympathetic-dominated pattern of autonomic response [p. 179]." The origin of neurosis (anxiety) may be related to a single, traumatic experience, to recurrent occasions of high anxiety, or to a chronic anxiety-evoking state of affairs. Furthermore, he argues for interventions like counterconditioning (including the use of assertive responses, deep relaxation, etc.) and extinction (including reactive inhibition).

g. Lazarus and Opton (1966) take the position that the stress response is a multidimensional concept, with components of physiologic arousal in the various organ systems, subjective phenomenology, and objective behavioral reactions. With regard to discrepancies between self-report (continuously measured during stress experience) and physiologic indicators (also continuously measured), they suggest an explanation in terms of defenses and social maneuvers to protect the self-esteem. In addition, physiologic adaptation occurs with repetition of stress circumstances, although this is probably not just a consequence of repetition. Also, adaptation requires time, but no one knows what psychologic events occur in adaptation. Using physiological indicators, they also report that highly anxious individuals show a reaction to the total experimental situation, rather than a reaction to the specifically designed threat inducers.

h. Mandler and Watson (1966) describe an interruption view of anxiety in which they argue that the interruption of an organized behavioral sequence will (under certain conditions) evoke anxiety. Anxiety occurs when no response is available whereby the arousal initiated by the interruption can be terminated, i.e., when interruption occurs and no alternative behavior is available (since this produces *helplessness* and *disorganization,* which describes anxiety). A number of factors influencing susceptibility to disruption are discussed, including: societal inculcation of well-organized plans for levels of achievement that most individuals actually cannot reach; expectations—e.g., prestress thinking about the stress coming up; competence, i.e., the ability to avoid disruption; frustration tolerance, i.e., being able to delay after interruption until appropriate substitute behavioral consequences can be found; degree of perceived control over the environment (i.e., locus of control); providing for alternate responses to stress or interruption; conflict, which activates and disrupts response sequences; defense mechanisms, which are attempts to avoid interruption; double-bind communication, which, as soon as it activates some organized sequence, interrupts it.

i. Spence and Spence (1966) propose that anxiety has D (i.e., drive) and S_D (i.e., drive stimulus) components, and that increases in "psychological stress," in addition to raising the drive level, initially increase task-attending behavior. But as anxiety increases in intensity, so does the frequency of task-irrelevant responses, and "to the extent that performance is adversely affected by them, these irrelevant tendencies will lead to performance decrement [p. 313]." They further suppose that the high-anxious individual has "a lower threshold for the arousal of anxiety than the low-anxious" individual. Going on, they state that: "Thus, while the performance of low anxiety groups would be expected to rise and then decline as stress increases, the period of initial rise in high anxiety groups, if it appears at all, would be expected to be attenuated and their decline in performance appear not only earlier on the stress continuum but be, at any given point, more pronounced [p. 314]."

j. Spielberger (1966), taking his cue from earlier studies (Cattell & Scheier, 1958, 1961), presents a trait-state conception of anxiety that is designed to distinguish between the "anxious person" (trait anxiety) and the person who is "anxious now" (state anxiety). Trait anxiety is assumed to reflect "past experience that in some way determines individual differences in anxiety-proneness, i.e., in the disposition to see certain types of situations as dangerous and to respond to them with state anxiety [p. 18]."

What these excerpts show is that there are many theories to explain the origins and manifestations of anxiety, and each deals with a somewhat different set of variables and concepts. But, taken together, they are more complementary than contradictory in what they say about anxiety, and their formulations converge at a number of points.

School Anxiety

The conceptual foundations of anxiety already discussed can now be focused upon the construct of school anxiety. The necessity for directing specific attention to the school setting is indicated by the work of two prominent groups of investigators. Atkinson has conceptualized anxiety in terms of an approach-avoidance paradigm, and relates anxiety to the need to avoid failure (Atkinson & Feather, 1966). The importance of this is that the school setting provides a natural laboratory in which many individuals are exposed to failure. The comprehensive series of studies of test anxiety by Sarason and his colleagues, which were guided by a psychoanalytic framework, have likewise shown the stressors operative in one selected category of school activities (Hill & S. B. Sarason, 1966; Sarason, Davidson, Lighthall, Waite, & Ruebush, 1960). Along with the issues detailed earlier, these point to the need for more systematic attention to anxiety in school settings.

A paradigm for school anxiety that has its origins in the nature of anxiety is presented in Figure 1. One purpose of the paradigm is to provide an overview of the classes of variables which are pertinent to a systematic consideration of school anxiety. In addition, the paradigm shows general relationships between different classes of variables, provides a rationale for interrelating the various studies to be reported in this book, suggests aspects of potential interventions in relation to anxiety in school, and ultimately helps to identify areas where research is lacking. It thus serves as a useful heuristic device.

Lazarus's (1966) theory of psychologic stress, in simplified form, states that once a stress condition has been appraised as threatening, coping processes occur "whose function it is to reduce or eliminate the anticipated harm." Three classes of factors are involved in this coping activity: the degree of threat, factors in the situation (e.g., the viability of certain types of actions), and factors in the person (e.g., his resources for dealing with the threat). The end results of these coping activities (as influenced by these factors) are reactions that, according to Lazarus, are behaviorally manifested as "affective experiences," "motor manifestations," "alterations in adaptive functioning," and "physiologic reactions." In addition, with the foregoing as constituents, there are different strategies, or patterns of reactions, including: anxiety reactions; actions aimed at strengthening the individual's resources against the anticipated harm; attack reactions (with or without the affect of anger); avoidance reactions (with or without the affect of fear); and various defensive tendencies.

In dealing with the effects of anxiety reactions in

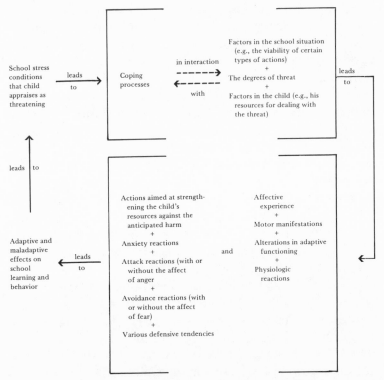

Figure 1.   School stress and anxiety paradigm

school it is important to differentiate between primary and secondary effects. In reference to the paradigm, the anxiety reaction may have its own maladaptive effects through its affective, motor, cognitive, and physiologic manifestations. But actions aimed at strengthening resources against anticipated harm, attack and avoidance reactions, and defensive tendencies may also have maladaptive effects in the school, and these effects may, in turn, become a new source of school stress and anxiety. Thus we see that many of the effects of anxiety in school are likely to be secondary effects, i.e., the result of the maladaptiveness of other reactions to stress (and their accumulation and incorporation in the personality of the child).

CHILDREN'S SCHOOL QUESTIONNAIRE (CSQ)

One source of data reported in this book was the Children's School Questionnaire (Phillips, 1966a), which consists of 198 questions read orally to children. Oral presentation was used to take advantage of intermediate-elementary age children's higher oral than reading comprehension level, the smaller variability at this age in oral comprehension (compared to reading comprehension), and the greater control over response rate, etc., which one has in oral administration. The items for the questionnaire were obtained from various sources, including the *Test Anxiety Scale for Children* (TASC) (Sarason, S. B. et al., 1960), the *Achievement Anxiety Scale* (Stanford, Dember, & Stanford, 1963), the *Audience Anxiety Scale* (Paivio, Baldwin & Berger, 1961), the *Defensiveness Scale for Children* (Lighthall, 1963), and the *Children's Personality Questionnaire* (Porter & Cattell, 1963). In addition, a large number of items were prepared by the author to measure aspects of achievement and social stress, and coping styles.

The items representing each of these categories were randomly split into thirds and assigned to Forms 1, 2, or 3 in a random order. After this was accomplished each form of the CSQ consisted of 66 items. One of the purposes in doing this was the practical necessity of dividing the time required for administration of all 198 items. As a result, each testing session lasted between 20 and 30 minutes, the time required depending on various factors, including the number of questions orally repeated. Another reason, however, was the desire to "randomize" as much as possible effects peculiar to a particular testing session, and effects associated with item position.

Procedures Used to Analyze CSQ Item Responses

Although items were included from instruments developed by others, this was not done so that scores derived from these particular items could be included in analyses. Instead, these pools of items were included as benchmarks. As an illustration of this strategy, the concept of school anxiety included anxiety associated with test and testlike situations, so it was likely that items of the TASC would constitute a core of items to which items tapping additional sources of school anxiety would adhere.

Since item responses were dichotomous, a correlation matrix was determined by computing phi coefficients, realizing, of course, that the size of phi was severely restricted in cases where proportions were extreme. However proportions above .8 and below .2 were the exception rather than the rule. This correlation matrix (R) then was converted to its G covariance matrix before a principal-components and a varimax rotation analysis, using a minimum eigen value of 1.00, were carried out. But before using these techniques it was necessary to decide whether to seek factors across the total sample, or factors common to particular subsamples, especially subsamples based on sex and sociocultural status. In terms of the general problems to be investigated, and the requirements of image and factor analytic techniques, it seemed that the most generally meaningful factors would be those derived from the total sample. So this is what was done.

This procedure was followed for CSQ data collected in 2 successive school years in order to check on the stability of the CSQ factor structure. To establish the degree of similarity between these factor structures, neither Ahmavaara's nor Kaiser's method of comparing factor structures could be used, for neither the same items nor the same subjects appeared in each of the image analyses. Instead, factors obtained on the two occasions were examined for common items with factor loadings of .40 or higher. It soon became apparent that four factors obtained on the first occasion were similar to four factors obtained on the second, since in each of these pairs of factors more than 75% of the items had loadings of .40 or higher on *both* factors (for school anxiety 90% did). Therefore, those items having .40 or higher loadings on the same factors on the two occasions were used to represent the factor. The items representing the school anxiety factor are shown in Table 1. It also should be pointed out that school anxiety "factor scores" were derived by assigning each item a weight of one and summing the item responses. The simplicity of this method of scoring, and the stability of the results obtained justified its use (Horn, 1965).

SCHOLASTIC VARIABLES

Sociometric nominations

Another source of data was children's nominations of other children in the classroom group for a series of five situations. The usual sociometric approach was employed except that both positive and negative choices were obtained, and choices were restricted to the same sex, i.e., boys chose only boys, and girls only girls. The reason for this latter decision is that status with one's own sex, expecially at this age level, is likely to be more discriminating than status with the opposite sex. With regard to obtaining both positive and negative nominations, there is evidence that a positive nomination is not simply opposite in meaning from a negative nomination (e.g., Phillips & DeVault, 1955). When asking for negative nominations, care was taken *not* to suggest that the children ought to make such nominations. This indirect, oblique approach is illustrated by the following item: "Suppose that the teacher selected someone to work with you; *if* there is someone you hope she won't select please write his name in the blank." With respect to peer status, therefore, there are two variables to be studied further: one is *peer acceptance* and the other is *peer rejection.*

Table 1 Items Representing the School Anxiety
Factor Found in Replicated Image Analyses of the CSQ

Form and item no.	Items
1-5*	Do you worry when the teacher says that she is going to ask you questions to find out how much you know? (2)
1-8*	Do you sometimes dream at night that you did poorly on a test you had in school that day?
1-10*	Do you worry a lot *while* you are taking a test? (2)
1-12	Is it hard for you to do as well as the teacher expects you to do in class? (3)
1-16*	Do you sometimes dream at night that the teacher is angry because you do not know your lessons? (4)
1-20	Do you often have the fear that other children might think you dumb?
1-27	Do you usually feel nervous when speaking to the principal?
1-30	Are you sometimes afraid of expressing yourself in class because you think you might make a foolish mistake? (3)
1-38	Are you often worried that the teacher will scold or punish you?
1-40	When it is your turn to get up and recite in class, do you feel your heart pounding hard?
1-42*	When you are at home and you are thinking about your arithmetic lesson for the next day, do you become afraid that you will get the answers wrong when the teacher calls upon you?
1-56*	Do you worry about being promoted, that is, passing from the _____ grade to the _____ grade at the end of the year? (2)
1-62*	Do you worry a lot *before* you take a test? (2)
1-63*	Do you think you worry more about school than other children?
1-65*	*After* you have taken a test, do you worry about how well you did on the test? (2)
1-66*	If you did very poorly when the teacher called on you, would you feel like crying, even though you would try not to cry?
11-3	Do you ever worry about knowing your lessons?

11-5*	When the teacher asks you to get up in front of the class and read aloud, are you afraid that you are going to make some bad mistake?
11-6	Do your knees shake when you are asked to recite in class? (4)
11-11	Do you sometimes have a fear of fainting in class? (4)
11-12*	When you are home and you are thinking about your reading lesson for the next day, do you worry that you will do poorly on the lesson?
11-14	Do you sometimes shake all over when you are asked to recite in class? (4)
11-16	When the teacher fails to notice and comment on your work does it make you unhappy?
11-17*	When you are in bed at night, do you sometimes worry about how you are going to do in class the next day?
11-20	Does your teacher sometimes give you a lower grade than you think you deserve?
11-26	Do you always feel uncomfortable when you do not know what is expected of you in class?
11-28*	Do you sometimes dream at night that you are in school and cannot answer the teacher's questions? (4)
11-33	Does your voice sometimes shake when you are asked to recite in class?
11-35	Is it hard for you to tell someone you're scared?
11-38	Do you have a hard time keeping up with the other students in class? (3)
11-45	If anything happens that tends to make you look foolish, do you tend to think about it for a long time afterwards?
11-46	Do you worry that you might forget your lines when you recite a poem in front of the class?
11-47	Do some of your friends think you are a sissy because you make good grades?
11-50	Do you dread choosing up sides to play games because you are usually one of the last ones chosen? (3)
11-52	Do you ever worry about something bad happening to someone you know?
11-53*	When you are taking a hard test, do you forget some things you knew very well before you started taking the test?
11-54*	Do you wish a lot of times that you didn't worry so much about a test? (2)

11-56*	When you are taking a test, does the hand you write with shake a little?
11-58	Have you ever been afraid of getting hurt?
11-63	Do the students that do poorly on the tests that the teacher gives lose the approval of the teacher?
111-2	If you think someone doesn't like you, does it bother you?
111-6	When someone is slow, does it bother you; or does it not bother you?
111-11	When you've done something wrong, is it hard for you to say you're sorry?
111-13	Do you sometimes worry about being different from many of the children in your class?
111-14	Do you usually feel awkward meeting new students who have just come into the class?
111-16*	When the teacher says that she is going to find out how much you have learned, does your heart begin to beat faster? (4)
111-17	Are you sometimes afraid of getting into arguments? (1)
111-19	Do some children in the class say things to hurt your feelings? (1)
111-22	Does it seem like most of the children in the class never pay any attention to you?
111-23*	When the teacher says that she is going to give the class a test, do you get a nervous or funny feeling?
111-25	Do you dislike reciting in class because you might make a mistake and others would laugh at you?
111-26	Do you ever worry about what is going to happen?
111-29	When one of your friends won't play with you, do you feel badly?
111-32	Is it hard for you to have as good a report card as your parents expect you to have? (3)
111-33	Do some children in the class seem to get angry when you do better than they do?
111-34	Are you afraid that other children will laugh at you when you show your work to them?
111-35	Are you frequently afraid you may make a fool of yourself? (1)
111-36*	Are you afraid of school tests?
111-39*	When the teacher says that she is going to give

	the class a test, do you become afraid that you will do poorly?
111-40	Do you worry a lot about your school work because you are afraid your parents might find out you are not doing as well as they expect you to do?
111-41	Do you ever worry about what people think of you? (1)
111-42	Do you feel nervous if the whole class watches you when you are making something?
111-43*	Do you sometimes dream at night that other boys and girls in your class can do things that you cannot do?
111-44	Do your classmates sometimes make fun of the way you look and talk? (1)
111-47	Do you feel nervous when others look at work you have done?
111-49*	When the teacher is teaching you about reading, do you feel that other children in the class understand her better than you?
111-50*	While you are on your way to school do you sometimes worry that the teacher may give the class a test?
111-52	Do you ever worry that you won't be able to do something that you want to do?
111-53	Are you often worried that you might be sick in class?
111-55*	While you are taking a test do you usually think you are doing poorly?
111-58*	When the teacher asks you to write on the blackboard in front of the class, does the hand you write with sometimes shake a little?
111-61	Do you feel cross and grouchy sometimes?
111-62	In your school work, do you often forget; or do you feel sure you can remember things? (3)
111-65	When you recite in class do you often wonder what others are thinking of you? (1)

NOTE: Items of the school anxiety factor marked with an asterisk (*) are in the TASC, and the six items representing each of the factorial dimensions of school anxiety are identified by the numbers in parentheses, with the factors marked as follows: 1 = Fear of Assertiveness and Self-Expression; 2 = Test Anxiety; 3 = Lack of Confidence in Meeting Expectations of Others; and 4 = Phsyiological Reactivity Associated with Low Tolerance of Stress.

Standardized Tests

The *California Test of Mental Maturity* (CTMM) and the *Metropolitan Achievement Test* (MAT) were used to obtain information on intellectual and academic functioning. The MAT was given by teachers, with minimal supervision, and scoring was performed by the author and his colleagues. The CTMM was given by the author and his colleagues with assistance from psychometric teams of the school system.

Teacher Grades

The grades reported by teachers in both subject matter and school conduct were utilized, even though there is considerable evidence that grades do not have the reliability and validity that researchers desire. Nevertheless, grades have been shown to be good predictors, especially when grades of two or more teachers are averaged, as was the case.

In addition, information on the previous school history of children was sought in the cumulative records in the schools. From this record, a number of different kinds of information was obtained, including teacher grades in preceding school years (grades 1–3), school attendance, and intelligence and achievement test data.

Teacher Nomination Forms

The use of teacher nominations of children for various traits was a major source of data. Such nominations probably are a measure of the teacher's value system regarding the classroom behavior of children, as well as being a measure of children's actual behavior in the classroom. It also is difficult to ascertain whether different teacher's nominations are comparable. But this is not just the problem of knowing whether children in different classrooms would receive comparable nominations. There is also the possibility that different classroom situations bring out different behaviors in different children. In spite of these limitations,

teacher's observations and judgments of the classroom behavior of children frequently have been significantly related to anxiety (Ruebush, 1963).

One instrument was designed to measure the desire
and effort to do well in school academically and socially,
and it is called *school motivation*. Some of the items designed
to measure desire and effort to do well in school academically were suggested by a study by S. B. Sarason, Davidson,
Lighthall, and Waite (1958), and those intended to measure desire and effort to do well in school socially were
developed by the author. Scores based on these two types
of items correlated about .80, so the items were subsequently combined into a single measure of school motivation. In devising the instrument, an attempt was made to
minimize the tendencies of some teachers to strongly skew
their distributions, and at the same time to allow room for
legitimate differences between classes.

Teacher nominations also were secured for a wide variety of different types of classroom behavior. One of the
major sources of these classroom "trait" characteristics is
the series of studies of problem behavior in school initiated
by Wickman (Stouffer & Owens, 1955; Wickman, 1928).
Forty of these trait characteristics were utilized in addition
to a number of other school behavioral characteristics that
were gleaned from other sources, especially the clinical
literature (Blanchard, 1946; Klein, E., 1949; Pearson,
1952). A total of 72 "items" were included in this problem
behavior instrument.

Teachers were asked to nominate the one or two children they associated with each of the characteristics or
school behavior traits described, and were asked to work
rapidly and freely, so that only children evidencing a
marked degree of a characteristic or trait received nominations (if it can be assumed that success was obtained in
getting the information desired from teachers). Such nominations were obtained on the same children over a period

of 2 consecutive years, on four different occasions, and nominations received by children on all four occasions were added together before image and factor analyses were performed. A G covariance matrix was first computed, and this was followed by a principal-components and a varimax rotation analysis.

Reliability of the Variables

In longitudinal studies, and studies of change, one is faced with a special problem that Bereiter (1963) referred to as the "unreliability-invalidity dilemma." As he points out, it is well known that, other things being equal, as the correlation between scores obtained on two different occasions increases, the reliability of the difference score decreases. At the same time, as the correlation between tests decreases, it becomes increasingly difficult to maintain that the tests are measuring the same thing. So, when one obtains a low correlation between pretest and posttest, he is faced with the problem of deciding whether conditions have changed so much for the posttest that the test is no longer measuring the same thing, or whether the experiences which have intervened between tests have not uniformly affected the scores of all subjects.

We have approached the problem of reliability of the variables in two ways. Our first concern was with homogeneity, and for this we relied on factorial techniques. For example, applying the KR 21 formula to the school anxiety items, values of .95 or higher were obtained.

There also was a small sample of teachers, randomly selected, who responded to the teacher problem behavior nomination and school motivation rating forms again about 1 week after the initial administration. Correlating the frequency with which children were nominated for problem behaviors, coefficients of about .90 were obtained. When instances in which children were nominated for the *same specific* problem behavior were examined, it was found that more than a third of the nominations were *identical*.

Test-retest correlations of about .90 also were obtained for the school motivation ratings.

In addition, we investigated the stability of the major variables across a period of 2 years. Since there was some attrition of subjects between occasions, as well as the addition of subjects between testing occasions and the absence of some subjects for particular tests, the same subjects were not available in the total sample on successive occasions. These correlation coefficients are presented in Table 2.

As might be expected, the stabilities declined as the

Table 2   Stabilities of Variables Across the 2 Years for Total Sample

Variable	Stability correlations					
	r_{12}	r_{13}	r_{14}	r_{23}	r_{24}	r_{34}
School motivation	67	58	50	55	54	54
School anxiety	63	59	52	74	64	68
Feelings of inferiority	28	13	13	10	11	47
Neurotic symptoms (academic)	40	27	26	25	19	42
Neurotic symptoms (social)	30	26	13	10	18	25
Aggression with independence strivings	47	27	37	25	31	49
Active withdrawal	34	18	27	27	34	44
Emotional disturbance with depression	45	21	26	43	45	44
Self-enhancement through derogation of others	39	23	26	30	41	48
Diffuse hyperactivity	41	26	30	36	43	47
Peer acceptance	47	44	43	49	46	59
Peer rejection	49	38	34	52	39	56
MAT nonverbal	82	74	76	76	78	80
MAT verbal	88	90	88	88	82	87
CTMM nonverbal	81	78	70	82	77	80
CTMM verbal	85	85	81	86	85	88
Grade-point average	83	70	67	69	68	82

NOTE: 1 = Beginning of 4th grade scores; 2 = End of 4th grade scores; 3 = Beginning of 5th grade scores; 4 = End of 5th grade scores. Decimal points are omitted.

length of time between testing periods increased. Obviously the highest stabilities were obtained with the objective tests, while the lowest were obtained with some of the problem behavior variables. Of course, these scores were based on only a few items. An additional factor regarding the problem behavior correlations across the summer months (i.e., r_{23}) is that different teachers and classroom groups were involved. Also, in comparing, for example, r_{12} with r_{13}, the correlations represent data obtained at different points in the school year.

FACTORIAL DIMENSIONS OF SCHOOL ANXIETY

The 74 items constituting school anxiety were subsequently image analyzed. Four factors were obtained in this analysis, and the six items with the highest loadings on each of these factors, and minimal loadings on the others, were selected as measures of each of these factors, as listed in Table 1. Factor 1 is identified as Fear of Assertiveness and Self-Expression; Factor 2 as Test Anxiety, which includes items from the TASC; Factor 3 as Lack of Confidence in Meeting Expectations of Others; and Factor 4 as Physiologic Reactivity Associated with Low Tolerance of Stress, which also includes some items from the TASC. Overall, 26 of the 30 items of the TASC are among the 74 items, and they generally had high loadings on the school anxiety factor. A further indication of this is that the correlation between test anxiety (based on 26 items) and school anxiety (based on 74 items) was .82, although such part-whole correlations are spuriously high. Using a formula (Guilford, 1965) for the correlation of a part (test anxiety) with a remainder (school anxiety minus test anxiety), a correlation of .61 was obtained. In addition, correlations were computed for the four factors, based on six items for each factor, over periods of time up to 2 years, with reliabilities in the .40s and .50s.

The multidimensional nature of the TASC has been reliably established by Dunn (1964, 1965) and Feld and Lewis (1967). Feld and Lewis included almost 7500 second graders in their factor analyses, which produced four factors. They identify these as Test Anxiety, Remote School Concern, Poor Self-Evaluation, and Somatic Signs of Anxiety. They further report that essentially the same factors were obtained for boys and girls.

A comparison of the items with the highest loadings on their factors with the items which have the highest loadings on our factors, makes it obvious that their Test Anxiety factor is the same as ours, and that their Remote School Concern and Somatic Signs of Anxiety factors are combined in our Physiologic Reactivity factor. Although a direct comparision of items for the other factors was limited, due to the lack of common items among the remaining factors, it is apparent that their Poor Self-Evaluation factor overlaps our Lack of Confidence in Meeting Expectations of Others and Fear of Assertiveness and Self-Expression factors.

In view of the marked differences in item pools analyzed (the school anxiety scale had 26 of the 30 TASC items *and* 48 additional items) and in the samples of children studied, this represents a surprising degree of overall similarity. As a result, it could be argued that the TASC might better be described as a measure of school anxiety, as Dunn (1968) has done. However, if it is assumed that there are four major components in school anxiety, as our series of factor analytic studies indicates, then it appears that our school anxiety scale (SAS) more adequately represents these components than does the TASC.

In more recent research, I. G. Sarason (1975b) has conceptualized two types of test anxiety: (1) that occurring in the context of generalized activity; and (2) that occurring in relation to isolated problems. In the former, the individual is characteristically anxious and worried in many areas, and has ambivalence and conflict over achievement and about being evaluated. In the latter, the individual is upset before, during, and after tests due either to inadequate learning or to specific unfortunate experiences (i.e., a traumatic event in the past).

Endler and O'Sada (1975) go further, taking the position that a person x situation model of anxiety *is necessary.* They have constructed a self-report test based on the assumption that anxiety is multidimensional, and that a measurement of it needs to be specific and congruent with threatening situations. Their inventory uses four general situations and includes nine modes or methods of response. The four situations are: (1) interpersonal, a situation involving interaction with other people; (2) physical danger, a situation where a person may encounter physical danger; (3) ambiguous or novel, which is a strange or new situation; and (4) general and daily, which is a situation involved in one's day-to-day routine.

Whether these conceptualizations, given that they are not entirely parallel to the anxiety studies reported, would through empiric analysis produce a factor structure similar to the ones described earlier, cannot be ascertained. However, both have an emphasis on situational factors, as does our conception and subsequent analyses of school anxiety, and both recognize the multidimensionality of anxiety. There also is the recognition that factors-in-persons contribute to the anxiety response.

NOTES

1. This section is based on an earlier summary of views of anxiety in Phillips, Martin, and Meyers (1972).

2. Izard later changed his position on this matter (see Spielberger, Ed., Vol. 1, 1972).

Chapter 2

THE NATURE OF SCHOOL STRESS[1]

Since anxiety is a reaction to stress, it is necessary to know something about settings that are likely to be stressful. Not only is it useful to know what kinds of situations are potentially stressful, but it is also important to know why they are stressful. In the light of such knowledge, the nature of school stress can be understood.

Psychologists, educators, and mental health theorists have given considerable attention to conceptualizing which situations are likely to be stressful. Caplan (1970) defines a crisis as a person's struggle with a current life stress. This may be related to a situation that challenges him beyond his current capacity, as is so often the case for children in school.

Among other theorists who have addressed these questions, Mandler and Watson (1966) suggest that it is the interruption of a person's plan of behavior that is stressful. An individual makes plans whose function is laying out a course or a sequence of behavior. Unanticipated interruptions of such a sequence of behavior produce a state of arousal (i.e., an undifferentiated stress response) followed by an emotional reaction, e.g., anxiety.

Freud (1949) postulates four major sources of tension (or stress), including frustration, conflict, threat, and physiologic growth processes; while other theorists view conflict as the major source of anxiety. In contrast, Rogers (Hall & Lindzey, 1957, p. 486) suggests that *any* experience that is inconsistent with the organization or structure of self may be stressful, and be perceived as a threat.

Erikson (1950) provides an excellent example of situations with high potential for stress with his eight development crises of man. Each of these stages specifies what psychologically important development must take place, and what will happen if it does not. For example, at school age the child must develop a sense of industry; if he does not he will be unable to compete successfully in society and will tend to feel inferior.

These delineations of potentially stressful situations are very gross, and are of limited use in identifying stressful situations in school. But Klein and Lindemann (1961) have developed three categories of potentially stressful situations that might be more helpful. First, there are those situations involving the loss or threatened loss of a significant relationship. Second, there are those situations involving the introduction of one or more new individuals into one's social orbit. Finally, there are those situations involving transitions in social status and role relationships as a consequence of maturation, achievement, or a new social role.

The list could be extended much further, because of the importance placed on stress and stress reactions in psychologic theory, but the views presented here are fairly representative of those that have been most influential. It should also be noted that the individual's own affective reactions to stress may, by a circular process, become an additional source of stress. Selye's (1956) account of the "general adaptation syndrome" shows how the effects of stress response can become self-perpetuating. Freud (1949) expresses similar concerns in his dynamic energy model of psychic conflict, by suggesting that the original conflict can deplete the energy the person has for coping with new instances of related or even unrelated stressors. But it is not only novel situations of rapid and unexpected onset that can lead to self-perpetuating stress response. Perhaps at least equally often it is stultifyingly familiar situations, in which one figuratively inhales his own prior scent of stress response, that become the occasions for repetition of the original noncoping behavior.

EXPERIMENTAL STRESS

One important aspect of anxiety has been the experimental manipulation of stress, and ego-involving instructions is one of the means of inducing psychologic stress. To induce stress the subject is informed that performance on an experimental task is related to intelligence, to other desirable personal qualities, or to success in school and in later life. The assumption is that such instructions tend to make subjects more attentive and involved in the task, and to be more concerned about doing well.

A number of studies, done mostly with college students, have shown that this form of instruction does increase stress (Denny, 1966; Nicholson, 1958; I. G. Sarason, 1961; Spielberger & Smith, 1966). However, one of the difficulties with the use of ego-involving instructions is that most experimental conditions are inherently involving. Therefore, results may occasionally be confounded by including nonstress conditions that are, in fact, stressful.

Nevertheless, one may conclude that ego-involving instructions are generally perceived as stressful, and this conclusion provides direct implications for stress in the classroom. We might consider, for example, whether and how the classroom environment tends to induce this type of stress. Clearly teacher behavior suggests that teachers attempt to use ego involvement to increase student performance. This is based on a middle-class assumption about what produces achievement. For children of lower-class background the techniques may not be ego involving.

There also is much research in which the experimental manipulation of failure has been used as a source of psychologic stress. A number of experimental studies have either induced actual failure or falsely reported failure to subjects. It usually has been found that this experience produces stress (Finch, Kendall, Montgomery, & Morris, 1975; Gordon & Berlyne, 1954; Marlett & Watson, 1968; I. G. Sarason, 1957; Walker, 1961). Again, the implications for the school environment are clearly discernible. For example, how does the school environment induce failure? In this connection, Proger, Mann, Taylor, & Morrell (1969) have demonstrated that testing every day produces significantly more stress than less frequent testing. And LeKarczyk and Hill (1969) have demonstrated significantly less stress as a result of "game" instructions when compared to traditional "test" instructions.

THE NATURE OF STRESSFUL SCHOOL SITUATIONS

This section focuses on school conditions, events, and interpersonal relationships, all of which are important sources of school stress. The information is obtained from items in the *Children's School Questionnaire* (Phillips, 1966a), indicative of two types of stressful situations. One of these involves achievement stressors, and the other concerns social stressors.

The information to be reported is obtained from responses of fourth graders in four elementary schools, one each serving middle-class Anglo, and upper-lower-class Anglo, and lower-class Black and Mexican-American children. Each school was highly homogeneous with respect to social class and racial/ethnic characteristics.

Some Sources of Achievement Stress

In Table 3 the proportions of middle-class (MC) Anglos, upper-lower-class (ULC) Anglos, and lower-class (LC) Blacks and Mexican-Americans who responded to these items in a stress direction have been tabulated. In most instances, stress is indicated by a "yes" response to the items. Where a "no" response has this meaning there is a special notation to that effect.

Almost 75% of the children say they often wish the teacher would slow down until they understand what she is saying better. In view of the reliance on verbal communication in teaching, this implies an important source of teacher ineffectiveness. It also is a significant source of achievement stress, since much verbal communication occurs in relation to academic work. As one might expect, this source of stress is strongest for Mexican-Americans, who have a language barrier (as well as primarily Anglo teachers), and it is weakest among MC Anglos.

Almost the same proportion also said that they work hardest when they know that what they do will be compared with what others in class do (Item 2-29). It is not surprising that so many say they work hardest under competitive conditions, since this agrees with much of the research evidence (e.g., Phillips, 1956). More importantly, it is obvious that a great deal of stress is inherent in the competitiveness that underlies so much schoolwork. The proportion who say this is highest among Blacks; it is significantly lower among Mexican-Americans. The latter result agrees with achievement socialization practices of Mexican-Americans.

Other items on which more than one-half of the children gave responses indicative of stress include 1-12, 2-27, 2-65, and 3-32. A majority of the children said that it was hard to do as well as the teacher expected them to do (Item 1-12). As might be expected, MC Anglos were less stressed this way than the other subgroups, although teacher expectations are a source of stress for almost 40% of this subgroup.

Making a mistake while reciting is more likely to cause some children to laugh among MC than ULC Anglos (Item 2-27). This is one of the two achievement stress items on which MC children indicate the highest stress. It also is sobering to realize that over half of all the children believe that making a mistake while reciting will lead to laughter by other children in class. Recitation, therefore, is likely to be a potent source of stress for many children.

All subgroups believe that smart children get privileges other children do not get (Item 2-65). Almost two-thirds believe this, which helps to explain the importance of tests to children, and the stressfulness of taking tests.

Having as good a report card as parents expect is a problem for over 60% of the children (Item 3-32). This stress is highest among Mexican-Americans, followed by the Blacks, and finally the MC Anglos. This fits well with studies showing that minority parents, especially Blacks, put strong pressure on their children for academic achievement (Katz, 1968). However, these pressures are not backed up by actions to translate these demands into success.

Less than a majority of the children gave responses indicative of stress to the remainder of the achievement stress items. Included among these items were the following conditions: children finding it hard to keep up with the rest of the class; children believing teachers sometimes give lower grades than they think they deserve; children believing some friends think they are a sissy because they made good grades; children believing that those who do poorly

Table 3 Proportions of Children Giving School Achievement Stress Responses

Item code	Item	MC Anglo (N=76)	ULC Anglo (N=95)	Mexican American (N=73)	Black (N=87)
1-12	Is it hard for you to do as well as the teacher expects you to do in class?	.39	.54	.53	.54
1-32	Do you find it hard to keep up with the rest of the class?	.27	.37	.53	.46
1-57	Do you often wish the teacher would slow down until you understand what she is saying?	.71	.76	.86	.78
2-20	Does your teacher sometimes give you a lower grade than you think you deserve?	.45	.54	.41	.57
2-27	If you made a mistake while reciting would some children laugh at you?	.70	.49	.55	.61
2-29	Do you work hardest when you know that what you do will be compared with what other students in class do?	.68	.76	.70	.82
2-38	Do you have a hard time keeping up with the other students in class?	.27	.42	.37	.34
2-47	Do some of your friends think you are a sissy because you make good grades?	.13	.14	.33	.14
2-63	Do the students who do poorly on the tests the teacher gives lose the approval of the teacher?	.34	.28	.48	.45
2-65	Do the children who are smart get privileges other children in class do not get?	.69	.59	.63	.63

38

3-9*	Do you get as much approval from the teacher in class as you would like to get?	.38	.39	.29	.32
3-27*	Do you expect to do better school work in the future than you have in the past?	.08	.11	.19	.15
3-32	Is it hard for you to have as good a report card as your parents expect you to have?	.55	.60	.84	.72
3-59*	Do you get as much approval from other children in class as you would like to get?	.38	.43	.38	.43

*"No" responses are scored. For all other items "yes" responses are scored.

NOTE: Size of differences between proportions of different subgroups required for significance at the .05 level ranges from .09 (for estimated population Ps near .90, .10) to .15 (for estimated population Ps near .50).

on their teacher's tests lose the teacher's approval; children saying they do not get as much approval from the teacher as they would like, as well as not getting as much approval from other children as they would like; and children not expecting to do better schoolwork in the future than they have in the past.

Good grades, as well as the things that appear to be associated with good grades, is a theme that obviously runs through these items—like teacher and peer approval, privileges, etc. On these items, Anglo children typically make fewer responses indicative of stress than do non-Anglo children. Since non-Anglos usually make poorer grades, this is a realistic difference. However, there are exceptions to this rule, particularly Items 2-20. 2-38, 2-47, and 3-9.

Overall, almost half of these children's responses to the achievement situations included in Table 3 were indicative of stress. And it is apparent that evaluation, and the things children see as being associated with evaluation, are central to achievement stress.

Some Sources of Social Stress

Social stress situations in school are presented in Table 4. Generally, the proportions are smaller than those for achievement stress, which is what one would expect to find because of the strong achievement orientation in elementary schools.

Differences between Anglo and non-Anglo subgroups are most pronounced on Items 1-48, 1-51, 1-58, 1-60, 2-37, 2-59, 3-33, and 3-44. However, non-Anglos have higher proportions on all but Item 1-58, which deals with whether a child's mother brings cookies, helps at class parties, and does other things like other children's mothers. This is a special problem of MC Anglo children, apparently because of the generally greater involvement of their parents. Where some parents are heavily involved, and others are relatively less involved in school, children are aware of and sensitive to these differences, and feel at a disadvantage.

Not surprisingly, more non-Anglo children, especially Blacks, report that they are physically attacked by other children. They also say that classmates often make fun of the way they play in school games. This is particularly true of Mexican-Americans. Non-Anglos also are more likely to believe that the clothes they wear to school are not as nice as what most children wear, and again the highest proportion occurs among Mexican-Americans.

More non-Anglos than Anglos claim that there are children in their classes who are unfriendly to them. Substantially more Mexican-Americans than other subgroups also report that they do not get along well with those children who are looked up to by the other children. Children who are looked up to usually get good grades, so that conflicts over the importance of being a good student, as revealed in responses to achievement stress, may be particularly acute among Mexican-Americans (especially boys).

Ironically, academic success is itself a source of stress

Table 4   Proportions of Children Giving School Social Stress Responses

Item code	Item	MC Anglo (N=76)	ULC Anglo (N=95)	Mexican American (N=73)	Black (N=87)
			Subgroups		
1-48	Have you been physically attacked by any children in class?	.22	.25	.45	.59
1-50*	Are you as good in games like kickball as other students in class?	.35	.39	.48	.39
1-51	Do your classmates often make fun of you for the way you play in school games?	.19	.32	.55	.38
1-52	Do you often feel that your classmates never want to do what you want to do?	.66	.46	.44	.52
1-55*	Do other children in class seem to like you?	.24	.18	.26	.21
1-58*	Does your mother bring cookies, help at class parties, and do other things like the mothers of the other children in class?	.41	.29	.22	.17
1-60*	Are the clothes you wear to school as nice as those most of the children wear?	.27	.21	.42	.36
2-36*	Does the teacher in class seem to like you?	.35	.17	.25	.18
2-37*	Are most of the children in class friendly to you?	.25	.21	.34	.33
2-59*	Do you get along well with those children in class who are looked up to by the other children?	.26	.24	.44	.25
3-19	Do some children in class say things to hurt your feelings?	.49	.47	.47	.51

3-22	Does it seem like most of the children in class never pay any attention to you?	.36	.33	.36	.41
3-28*	Do you get along well with the teacher in class?	.18	.16	.11	.18
3-33	Do some children in class seem to get angry when you do better than they do?	.34	.33	.59	.52
3-44	Do your classmates sometimes make fun of the way you look and talk?	.29	.28	.49	.38

*"No" responses are scored. For all other items "yes" responses are scored.
NOTE: Size of differences between proportions of different subgroups required for significance at the .05 level ranges from .09 (for estimated population Ps near .90, .10) to .15 (for estimated population Ps near .50).

for many children, as revealed in Item 3-33. The proportion is highest among Mexican-Americans again, but even a third of the Anglo students say this is what they believe, too. Thus about 40% of all children create stress for themselves whenever they are academically successful in school. And teachers, who generally are dedicated to the encouragement of excellence, may not be aware that one of the effects of their efforts is to create a "boomerang effect" on successful children that hits hardest at minorities.

Some Further Observations on Achievement and Social Stress

The sharpest delineation between MC and ULC Anglos occurs with respect to Items 1-12, 2-38 (Table 3), 1-51, 1-52, 1-58, and 2-36 (Table 4). And of these, MC Anglos appear to be more vulnerable to stress in relation to: feelings that classmates never want to do what they want to do; beliefs that their mothers do not bring cookies, help at class parties, and do other things like the mothers of other children in class; and beliefs that their teachers do not like them. On the other hand, ULC Anglos are more vulnerable to stress in relation to: beliefs that it is hard to do as well in class as their teachers expect them to do; beliefs that they have a hard time keeping up with other children in class; and beliefs that classmates often make fun of the way they play in school games.

Thus the ULC Anglo child appears to experience stress in terms of his deficiencies, especially in relation to achievement demands, and is more concerned about the avoidance of failure. In contrast, social norms seem to be more the basis of the stress of the MC Anglo child, who seems more preoccupied with achieving success, especially socially, rather than avoiding failure. In the terminology of Atkinson (Atkinson & Feather, 1966), the MC child is approach oriented, and the ULC child is avoidance oriented, in their school behavior.

Blacks and Mexican-Americans represent two distinct lower-class minorities in the school. Although these groups share characteristics associated with lower-class status, they represent different subcultures, and also differ in response to school stress Items 2-20, 2-29, 2-47 (Table 3), 1-48, 1-51, 2-59, and 3-44 (Table 4).

Blacks evidence more stress than Mexican-Americans in relation to: believing teachers sometimes give them lower grades than they deserve; saying that they work hardest when they know that what they do will be compared with what other students in class do; and indicating that they have been physically attacked by other children in class. Mexican-Americans indicated more stress in relation to: believing that some of their friends think they are a sissy because they make good grades (applicable mostly to boys); believing that classmates often make fun of them for the way they play in school games; believing that they do not get along well with children in class who are looked up to by other children; and believing that classmates sometimes make fun of the way they look and talk.

While the stress situations of Black children seem to involve achievement aspirations and physical aggression, those of Mexican-American children seem to be more related to sex role (especially masculinity) and personal appearance and speech patterns. The extent to which these are culturally induced is at this time only conjectural, but this is a promising line of further inquiry.

Conclusions

This phenomenologic analysis of stressors in the school environment has pointed up the possibility of establishing normative environmental probability rates for stressors that can differentiate in a lawful way among susceptible populations. It also has shown in general that risk rates differ for persons belonging to different subsets of the population, leading to the expectation that the actual relationship between particular sets of child characteristics and stress response will vary as a function of membership group. Further, the results reinforce the perspective of Katz (1968) on school stress among Blacks.

SCHOOL STRESS IN RELATION TO TRAIT AND STATE ASPECTS OF ANXIETY

Spielberger's (1972) concept of state anxiety is based on the critical role of stress associated with the situation or condition to which the person is exposed. In his paradigm, (Stress → Perception of danger [threat] → Increase in State Anxiety), stress refers to the objective stimulus properties of a situation, and threat refers to an individual's perception of that situation as more or less dangerous or threatening to him. If stress and threat are present, an increase in anxiety-state (A-State) is likely to occur. Another way to conceptualize the process is that if A-State is heightened in an individual, then he has perceived a situation or condition (he has been exposed to) as threatening to him. Thus it seems logical that if a group of individuals are exposed to a common situation, the overall frequency and intensity of arousal of A-State reported by those individuals may be used to determine the "objective stress value" of that particular situation or condition. This approach to determine or infer stress values of certain situations related to school experience has been employed in an unpublished study by Pannu (1974).

The situations selected for inclusion in the study, which are listed in Table 5, represent *salient* situations, i.e., those commonly referred to in anxiety questionnaires for school children, and were situations involving possible threat to self-esteem or ego (used for theoretic reasons, since this is an important characteristic of many anxiety theories). In addition, only the anticipated aspects of each

Table 5   Rank Order of the Situations According to Their Stress Values as Determined by A-State Means

Rank order	Brief descriptions of situations	A-State Means (total sample)
1	Being in the principal's office waiting for him to return	15.40
2	Being asked to stand in front of the class and share some information	12.34
3	About to take a test	12.19
4	Being asked by parents to show report card	11.62
5	Being told by teacher that what you do would be compared with what the other children in class do	11.53
6	A situation in which one of the most popular children in class is going to have a party at home but not all the children would be invited to it, and invitations are about to be passed out	11.48
7	A situation in which only half of the class is going to the kindergarten class to help the children, and the teacher has started calling out the names of the children she has selected to go with her	10.72

situation were referred to, again for theoretic reasons, since it is the anticipation of a dangerous or harmful experience that is most stressful, rather than the actual experience of the situation.

Using Spielberger's procedures for measuring A-State, with adaptations to meet the needs of this particular study, the results shown in Table 5 were obtained, with a sample of 330 fourth-, fifth-, and sixth-grade children in a predominantly lower class, Mexican-American school, a predominantly lower class Anglo school, and a predominantly middle class Anglo school, all in a semi-rural central Texas community.

Using Duncan's *Multiple Range Test,* the situation pertaining to the principal was clearly by itself in stress value, followed by the situations involving taking a test and speaking in front of the class, and then by the report card, peer competition, and peer-rejection situations. The possible teacher-rejection situation was clearly the least stressful.

To summarize other major results, there also were the following highly significant interactions: A-Trait X Situations, Sex X Situations, Ethnicity X Situations, Socioeconomic Status (SES) X Situations, and School X Situations. Consistent with A-State vs A-Trait theory, children differing in levels of anxiety proneness showed greater differences on A-State in situations low in stress values, and progressively less differences for situations higher in stress values.

Sex differences in A-State were most pronounced on the possible teacher-rejection and test-taking situations, with boys being higher on the former and girls on the latter. With respect to ethnicity, Anglos were higher in A-State on the talking-in-front-of-class and the principal's-office situations, while Mexican-Americans were generally higher on the others. School differences were most pronounced on the talking-in-front-of-class, peer-competition, and possible teacher-rejection situations. On all three of these situations the lower-class Anglo school had the highest and the middle-class Anglo school had the lowest A-State scores.

Two highly significant and intriguing interactions also occurred with respect to A-State, involving SES and School factors in interaction with ethnicity. These results are represented in Figures 2 and 3.

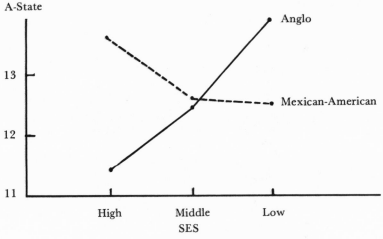

Figure 2.   A-State means for SES X Ethnicity
interaction effect on A-State

We see in Figure 2 that low-SES Mexican-American children had lower A-State than low-SES Anglo children, while the reverse was true among high-SES children. We see a further reversal of this phenomenon, however, when the school is taken into account. Mexican-American children (mostly lower-class) in a predominantly lower-class Anglo school are more A-State anxious (i.e., they see school situations as generally more stressful) than their lower-class Anglo counterparts, while Mexican-American children (mostly lower class) in a predominantly lower-class, Mexican-American school are less A-State anxious than their Anglo (mostly lower-class) counterparts.

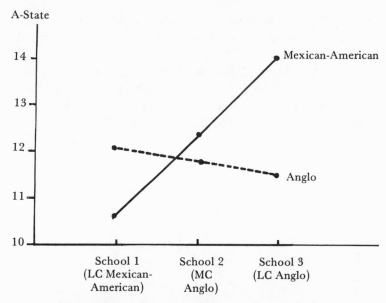

Figure 3.   A-State means for Ethnicity × School interaction effect on A-State

In summary, the significance of these results in terms of school stress, is:

1.   Socioeconomic background of children is a more influential factor than ethnic background in school stress.

2.   Minority status in a school (defined as being in the minority, regardless of racial-ethnic status) seems to be an important factor in school stress, with such status leading to higher stress.

3.   Individual school practices influence stress, so that some prototypic situations elicit more stress in some schools than in others.

4.   Knowledge such as this is important in school intervention, since without thorough individual, group, situational, and school-level diagnosis, the chances of successful intervention to eliminate or modify stress and-or anxiety are seriously compromised.

SELF-DISCLOSURE AND SUBJECT-ROLE STRESS, AND COPING STYLES

Self-report instruments are widely used by psychologists and educators in the schools, and it has been well documented that factors such as acquiescence and social desirability are embedded in responses to such instruments. The background for the present research is a conceptualization of such tendencies in terms of self-disclosure and subject-role stress, and the styles of coping with such stress that children manifest (Phillips, 1966a, 1971). The essentials of the theory are schematically represented in Figure 4.

The theory assumes that acquiescence is primarily a response to stress associated with self-disclosure *conditions*, while social desirability is primarily a response to stress associated with the *content* of self-disclosure. It is further assumed that many children react principally in terms of the stress of these situational factors, *or* they react in terms of the content of the items. This point of view is supported by the lack of a relationship between acquiescence and social desirability, and by the fact that these variables usually emerge as separate factors (Fiske & Pearson, 1970; Wiggins, 1968).

Acquiescence and social desirability can be delineated further by using two types of items. Type A represents socially *desirable* characteristics *few* children have, and Type B represents socially *undesirable* characteristics *most* children have. The tendency to agree with Type A *and* B items represents "acquiescence," and the tendency to disagree is labeled "negativism." Contrariwise, the tendency to agree with Type A items and to disagree with Type B items represents "self-enhancement," since this pattern of responding makes a person "look good." The opposite pattern of responding is labeled "self-criticalness."

It also may be assumed that children's prior stressful

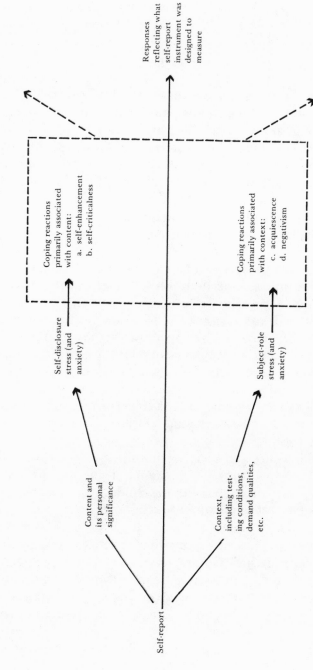

Figure 4. Schematic representation of "overt" and "covert" responses to self-reports

Responses reflecting what self-report instrument was designed to measure

Coping reactions primarily associated with content:
a. self-enhancement
b. self-criticalness

Coping reactions primarily associated with context:
c. acquiescence
d. negativism

Self-disclosure stress (and anxiety)

Subject-role stress (and anxiety)

Content and its personal significance

Context, including testing conditions, demand qualities, etc.

Self-report

school experiences contribute to their reactions to the self-reporting process. If the stress they experience in school is primarily interpersonal in nature, they are likely to be oversensitive to the threat inherent in the subject-role and demand qualities of the self-report *situation.* But if they are primarily "stressed" by the academic aspects of schooling, they are likely to be oversensitive to the threat inherent in the pervasively negative self-evaluative nature of the *content* of most self-report instruments.

Obviously, this is a somewhat different conceptualization of such response variance, but the experimental study of stress (e.g., Lazarus, 1966) does seem to support the rationale. In addition, the rationale assumes only that causality is *predominantly* from stress to coping reaction, and leaves open the question of whether there are other stress reactions besides the four identified. It also says nothing about factors-in-persons which might induce one type of reaction in preference to another.

As to the significance of these coping styles, it has been shown by Phillips (1971) that they are related to teacher and peer appraisals, objective measures of achievement and ability, and to problem behaviors in school. A summary of these findings appears in Table 6.

What the results show is that teacher and peer appraisals, and problem behaviors, differentiate acquiescent from negativistic children, but not self-enhancing from self-critical children. Overall, negativistic children have lower teacher and peer appraisals and exhibit more problem behavior than acquiescent children. In contrast, self-enhancing children have lower means on all four of the school achievement and ability measures than self-critical children, while none of these differences between negativistic and acquiescent children reaches statistical significance. Thus it would appear that children who have different styles of coping with self-report stress generalize such tendencies to a wide variety of other school situations. In addi-

Table 6 Scholastic Behavior Means of Acquiescent vs. Negativistic, and Self-Enhancing vs. Self-Critical Children

Variables	Acqui-escent	Nega-tivistic	P (F test)	Self-enhanc-ing	Self critical	P (F test)
Teacher and peer appraisals						
Grade-point average	12.3	11.4	.01	11.5	12.1	.26
School motivation	25.5	22.5	.05	25.2	23.2	.08
Peer acceptance	.26	.21	.04	.22	.19	.57
Peer rejection	.21	.26	.02	.27	.24	.63
School achievement and ability						
MAT NV	3.7	3.6	.14	3.5	3.9	.01
MAT V	4.0	3.7	.07	3.8	4.4	.01
CTMM NV	102.4	99.7	.19	96.5	104.6	.01
CTMM V	100.4	97.2	.13	94.7	104.1	$<$01
Problem behavior						
Feelings of inferiority	.50	.62	$<$01	.64	.54	.59
Neurotic symptoms (academic)	.56	.65	.56	.93	.78	.54
Neurotic symptoms (social)	.53	.70	.01	.74	.92	.28
Aggression with In-dependence strivings	.32	.88	$<$01	.67	.49	.60
Active withdrawal	.62	.94	.02	.61	.88	.11
Emotional disturbance	.30	.36	.53	.37	.74	.04
Self-enhancement through derogation of others	.26	.26	.94	.38	.22	.14
Diffuse hyper-activity	.26	.46	.02	.35	.39	.70

NOTE: This table taken from Phillips (1971)

tion, it appears that acquiescence and self-criticalness are more adaptive forms of coping than negativism and self-enhancement, at least in school situations.

Gotts, Adams, and Phillips (1968–1969) identify two school-related dimensions along which children's school behaviors vary, which may be a useful model for conceptualizing the relation of coping styles to school adjustment and performance. The two dimensions are: active versus passive, and noncoping versus interpersonal coping. If these dimensions are assumed to be unrelated, they form four subgroups, as shown in Figure 5, which is taken from Gotts, Adams, and Phillips (1968–1969).

Although the overlap is not complete, the school behavior characteristics of these subgroups are in important

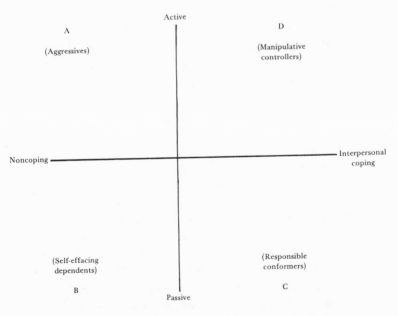

Figure 5. The empiric school coping and activity dimensions

ways similar to those found for the stress coping style subgroups. The "aggressives" are similar to negativistic children, the "self-effacing dependents" to self-enhancing children, the "manipulative controllers" to the self-critical children, and the "responsible conformers" are similar to acquiescent children. There is one apparent discrepancy, though, and this is in the alignment of the self-effacing dependent subgroup with the self-enhancing subgroup. The problem here may be that the activity and coping dimensions represent overt behaviors, while stress coping styles represent more covert behaviors.

From this analysis it would appear that negativistic children are least capable of adapting to the interpersonal setting of the elementary school. They are closely followed by self-enhancing children, with the exception that this subgroup receives high school motivation ratings from their teachers. In contrast, self-critical children are the most capable of adapting to academic demands, but adapt poorly to the interpersonal setting. Overall, acquiescent children show the best adjustment to school.

Cross-Cultural Significance of Coping Styles

The generality and significance of coping styles also is evident in research conducted in other countries and cultures. In one such study[2] the incidence of coping styles among Indian (Punjab state), Malaysian, and Chinese (Malaysian) children was investigated. At the same time, relations between coping styles and age, sex, and socioeconomic status were examined.

The Malaysian sample was obtained from classes in which Malay or English was the language (medium) of instruction.[3] Only Malay pupils are in Malay medium classes, while the English medium classes are mixed, having both Malay and Chinese children. Subjects were obtained from grades (standards) 3, 4, 5, and 6, including eight English medium classes and six Malay medium classes. Altogether, there were 200 Chinese subjects and 407 Malay subjects in the sample, ranging in age from 9 to 12, excluding the small number of Indians and others in the original sample. This sample was selected to be representative of these two cultural subgroups in Malaya, but it cannot be considered to be representative of the Malayan children's population as a whole. Socioeconomic status (SES) was based on father's occupation, and the four classifications were: 1 = professional and high administrative, 2 = subprofessional and business, 3 = clerical and skilled, and 4 = unskilled.

The Indian sample was obtained from a medium and a large (population over 100,000) city in Punjab state.[4] There are colleges in both of the cities and three schools in each city were used. Of these six schools, two were girls' schools, one a boys' school, and three coeducational schools. The criterion for determining SES was parents' income ($2000 to $5999 per year = lower SES; and $6000 and up = higher SES). The sample consisted of 371 lower-SES subjects and 323 upper-SES subjects, ranging in age from 10 to 16. The sample was selected to be representative of the urban area of Punjab state, but due to the sociocultural diversity of India it is unlikely to be representative of India as a whole.

The basic results are shown in Table 7. Overall, almost half of the total sample exhibited coping behavior, and the proportion of "copers" showed only small variation across culture, sex, age, and socioeconomic status. Broken down into types of "copers," 37% were acquiescent, 36% were self-critical, 16% were negativistic, and 12% were self-enhancing. In contrast, for American children the results were: acquiescent = 37%, self-criticalness = 16%, negativistic = 25%, and self-enhancing = 22%. Another comparison can be made by looking at the percentage for self-disclosure vs. subject-role stress. The figures are 47% and 53% respectively, for Indian-Malaysian children, and

Table 7 Frequency of Different Types of Stress Responses for Subjects Classified by Culture, Age, Sex, and Socioeconomic Status (SES)[1]

Source of stress response	Type of stress response	Culture			Age				Sex		SES		Total sample
		Indian (Punjab state)	Malay	Chinese (Malaysian)	9,10	11,12	13,14	15,16	Boys	Girls	High	Low	
Subject role stress	Acquiescence	139	45	13	52	73	45	26	89	108	80	117	197
	Negativism	23	33	29	31	34	8	5	52	33	37	48	85
	Combined	162	78	42	83	107	53	31	141	141	117	165	282
Self-disclosure stress	Self-enhancement	30	24	10	31	25	6	2	37	27	31	33	64
	Self-criticalness	116	47	28	36	90	41	10	115	76	89	102	191
	Combined	146	71	38	67	115	47	12	152	103	120	135	255
Total stress-response subjects		308	149	80	150	222	100	43	293	244	237	300	537
Total non-stress response Ss		387	234	123	233	337	104	70	432	312	307	437	744
Total sample		695	383	203	383	559	204	113	725	556	544	737	1281
Stress response subjects as percent of total sample		44.3	38.9	39.4	39.2	39.7	49.0	38.1	40.4	43.9	43.6	40.7	41.9

* The original total combined sample was 1301, but 42 subjects were excluded from the age analysis, and 20 subjects were excluded from the culture, sex, and SES analyses.

38% and 62% for American children. The major deviation from the American results, therefore, is that self-critical-ness is much more common in the Indian-Malaysian sample, which seems compatible with much that is written about the "Asian mentality."

One of the most important findings was that coping reactions to subject-role stress varied markedly across culture, age, and sex. Acquiescent coping dominated among Indian (Punjab state) children, while negativism was more common among Chinese (Malaysian) children. Acquiescence also increased with age, and was relatively more frequent among girls. Overall, it would appear that these children respond more passively to external stimuli (i.e., the context), while boys and Chinese (Malaysian) subjects respond in a more actively disengaging manner. In contrast, coping reactions to self-disclosure stress varied only across age. Self-enhancement usage declined, and there was a peaking of self-criticalness in the 11–14 age period. This corresponds to the period of puberty for many children, and an increased self-critical tendency seems compatible with developmental aspects of this period.

In conclusion, the results give further support to the theory espoused earlier, and to the interpretation of certain response biases as coping behavior. In addition, such coping behavior has obvious crosscultural as well as developmental implications.

NOTES

1. Some portions of this chapter are based on an earlier analysis of school stress by Phillips, Martin, and Meyers (1972).

2. This study was conducted in cooperation with Shyam L. Ahuja, a native of India, who returned to India for the purpose of this study, Norman Charles Harris, and Ng See Ngean, a professor at The University of Malaya, who carried out that part of the study.

3. Ng See Ngean, University of Malaya, did this part of the study.

4. Shayam Lata Ahuja returned to India to do this part of the study. Along with a fifth grade teacher, an English teacher, and a Hindi teacher, she translated the instruments used. The Hindi version was retranslated into English to be sure the translated version conveyed the exact meaning, because some items needed to be adapted. Similar procedures were used by Ng See Ngean in the Malaysian portion of the study, although an adapted English version was used in the English medium classes.

Chapter 3

ANXIETY IN THE ELEMENTARY SCHOOL[1]

The correlates and implications of school anxiety are extensive, diverse, and of great scope, as illustrated by the studies reported in this chapter. In the first three of these, relationships are charted between school anxiety and teacher and peer appraisals, school problem behavior, and school achievement. In a related study, the relation of school anxiety to under- and overachievement is investigated. In the next study, relations between school anxiety and masculinity-femininity are analyzed. These are examined both in terms of tests and overt behaviors that reflect the interpersonal side of the child's personality. In another related study, school anxiety is examined as a source of variation in children's interpersonal preferences as determined through sociometric choice. This is followed by reports of sex, social class, and racial-ethnic status differences in school anxiety, and an analysis of their educational significance. From the breadth of these phenomena, in which school anxiety appears as a source of individual differences, the construct's importance in adaptive-maladaptive school behavior is, therefore, further established.

TEACHER AND PEER APPRAISALS

School situations may be characterized in terms of the social and academic stress (and threat) they produce. Social threat refers to social aspects of school situations that tend to elicit anticipations of danger or harm. Typically, social threat is associated with teacher and peer rejection, hostility, and avoidance, or with the lack of acceptance, friendliness, and cooperativeness by teachers and peers. The degree to which social threat exists is likely to be associated with (a) the degree of cognitive uncertainty about the outcomes of such social encounters, (b) the amount of rejection or lack of acceptance by teachers and peers, and (c) the status and power of teachers and peers.

Similarly, academic threat refers to academic aspects of school situations which elicit anticipations of harm and psychologic danger. However, whether a high expectancy of failure is itself sufficient to produce threat is conjectural. For example, in Atkinson's formulation (Atkinson & Feather, 1966) fear of failure would decrease as the subjective probability of failure increased beyond .50. But as Katz (1968) points out, Atkinson's rationale deals only with the component of incentive strength that is determined by the apparent difficulty of the task. Although not specifically directed at the issue raised here, S. B. Sarason et al. (1960) stress the importance of anticipated disapproval by parents, teachers, and peers on the negative valence of fear of failure. Presumably, the child's own perception of the difficulty of tasks is relatively unaffected by the degree to which he believes that failure to meet prevailing standards of achievement will bring adult and peer disapproval. In these circumstances, fear of parental, teacher, and peer disapproval is likely to increase as failure becomes more probable.

In Table 8 correlations between school anxiety and teacher and peer appraisals vary widely. Therefore, if such appraisals contribute to a higher level of anxiety, the extent of this contribution varies by sex and sociocultural status. For example, no correlations approach significance among MC Anglo boys, but three of four are significant among MC Anglo girls. In contrast, three are significant for upper-lower class (ULC) Anglo boys but none for girls. Added to this, only one of the eight correlations is significant for Black boys and girls. There is reason to doubt, therefore, that school anxiety is a direct function of the stress inherent in teacher and peer appraisals.

SCHOOL PROBLEM BEHAVIOR

Some investigators have held that since a child's main school motivation is to find a place for himself in his classroom group, lack of acceptance leads to increasingly socially destructive aims and, eventually, to hopelessness and withdrawal (e.g., Dreikurs, 1968). Thus the interpersonal setting is the crucible in which the child works out his destiny, for teacher and peer appraisals not only indicate his school success and failure, they indicate to him something more important—the place he has in the classroom group.

Schachter (1959) notes several consequences of social isolation pertinent to social isolation in classroom groups. Although Schachter's discussion is primarily in terms of being isolated physically from others so that social contacts are not possible, our concerns deal with isolation in the sense of not being psychologically visible to, or of being ignored and avoided by, members of the group. In this latter context, social isolation through avoiding, ignoring,

Table 8 Correlations between School Anxiety and Teacher and Peer Appraisal

	MC Anglo		ULC Anglo		Mexican-American		Black	
Variable	*Boys* (N = 76)	*Girls* (N = 76)	*Boys* (N = 47)	*Girls* (N = 55)	*Boys* (N = 63)	*Girls* (N = 67)	*Boys* (N = 43)	*Girls* (N = 41)
School Motivation		−30†	−16	−18	−19	−12	−15	
Grade-point average		−33†	−45†		−37†	−26*	−31*	
Peer acceptance		−25*	−36*	−11	−31*	18		
Peer rejection		19	44†		25*	13	11	18

* Significant at .05 level
† Significant at .01 level
NOTE: Correlations less than .10, and decimals, omitted

or rejecting will lead to two types of consequences. The first is the experience of anxiety and other stress (threat) reactions, and this would be followed by a diminution or a heightened tempo of activity. It is anticipated that these changes in activity would be, in many instances, classed as underachievement and problem behavior by teachers and peers.

Kissell (1965) supports this view, and in a related study, Bovard (1959) hypothesizes that social isolation increases vulnerability to stress. But the socially isolated and rejected person is denied the opportunity to affiliate, and thus becomes more anxious.

Individuals who are anxious also are disposed toward being threatened by novel, strange, and unfamiliar circumstances, and thus ought to prefer well-explored milieus and familiar situations. If the anxious person has a reduced scope of functioning in his milieu, he might be expected to engage in more fantasy or daydreaming activity, and in studies using several different anxiety measures, the frequency of daydreaming has been consistently positively related to anxiety (Reiter, 1963; Singer & Rowe, 1962; Singer & Schonbar, 1961). Also, high-anxious students develop problem-solving techniques in groups later and show less leadership than low-anxious students (Cohen & Forest, 1968).

According to S. B. Sarason and his colleagues (1960), children who experience anxiety in evaluative situations are reacting with strong unconscious hostility to the evaluators, whom they believe are (or will be) in some way passing judgment on their adequacy. This hostility is in conflict with their dependency needs and is not openly expressed, but is frequently turned against the self in the form of self-derogatory attitudes. This strengthens the expectations of failure and children's desire to escape such situations, and leads to impairment of functioning.

Subsequently, when these children's behavior is observed in school situations, it is frequently described as dependent, direction-seeking, conforming, and occasionally as markedly unresponsive (S. B. Sarason, 1966). In some circumstances, however, it may be overtly directed at others, i.e., teachers, parents, and peers, although Sarason believes that few anxious children overtly behave in a hostile and aggressive manner. It is his impression that in these cases, "hostile and aggressive behavior are consequences of the lack of success of dependent tendencies."

With respect to school problem behavior, two opposing expectations can be generated from this review of the literature. One is that anxious children will not manifest higher levels of problem behavior, since most such behavior is overt and involves "acting out" in many forms, and is pervasively aggressive and hostile in nature. The other expectation is that many anxious children, especially boys and minorities, are conditioned to give overt expression to their fears, apprehensions, and concerns. This would lead to a tendency for anxiety to be positively related to the incidence of school problem behavior.

Correlations between anxiety and school problem behavior are presented in Table 9. Taking the correlations as a whole, the effects of anxiety are significant only in scattered instances. Generally, therefore, it appears that Sarason and his colleagues are right. Children who are anxious in school do not typically behave in an "acting-out," hostile, and aggressive manner. Of course, there may be other maladaptive school behaviors related to children's anxiety that are not adequately reflected in the problem behaviors sampled.

ANXIETY AND ACADEMIC ACHIEVEMENT

Low negative correlations (on the order of .30–.40) between anxiety and intelligence and academic achievement

Table 9 Correlations between School Anxiety and Problem Behaviors

Variable	MC Anglo		ULC Anglo		Mexican-American		Black	
	Boys (N = 76)	Girls (N = 76)	Boys (N = 47)	Girls (N = 55)	Boys (N = 63)	Girls (N = 67)	Boys (N = 43)	Girls (N = 41)
Feelings of inferiority			27	15				
Neurotic symptoms (academic		40†	11	16	24			12
Neurotic symptoms (social)	19			16		−20		−12
Aggression with independence strivings			31*		−12		30*	31*
Active withdrawal	19	30†	29*	15			18	
Emotional disturbance with depression		24*	16	16		13		
Self-enhancement through derogation of others			17				24	
Diffuse hyperactivity		10	10	13	−10	−14	28	12

*Significant at .05 level
†Significant at .01 level
NOTE: Correlations less than .10, and decimals, omitted

65

are a consistent finding in the majority of investigations, although relationships are higher in studies of children (Ruebush, 1963). In addition, more consistent results have been found when the TAS or TASC was used as the measure of anxiety, than when the MAS or CMAS was used (Forbes, 1969; S. B. Sarason et al., 1960; I. G. Sarason & Minard, 1962; I. G. Sarason, 1963).

The relationship between anxiety and intelligence and academic achievement is particularly important because of its causal implications. For example, does a substantial negative relationship indicate that those who are intelligent and high achievers are more capable of coping with their environment and are, therefore, less anxious?

S. B. Sarason et al. (1960) take the position that anxiety is the etiologically significant factor. One of the arguments on which their case rests is that the relation between anxiety and intelligence and academic achievement test performance depends on the situational context. That is, when a test is administered in a highly testlike atmosphere the relationship obtained is greater than when a more neutral, relaxed atmosphere is achieved (Zweibelson, 1956).

Another argument for interpreting anxiety as the causal factor involves the comparison of high- and low-anxious children's achievement performance when the effects of intelligence are controlled. Waite, Sarason, Lighthall, and Davidson (1958) matched high- and low-anxious children on the basis of intelligence, but found that low-anxious subjects still learned more rapidly on a paired associate learning task. In another study, K. S. Davidson (1959) found a significant negative relationship, limited to boys, between grades in school and anxiety, with intelligence held constant. In addition, Taylor (1964) reviewed the literature from 1933 to 1963 and found that anxiety differentiated overachievers from underachievers. Sarason and his colleagues (Hill & Sarason, 1966; Sarason, Hill, & Zimbardo, 1964) have also reported that changes in test anxiety across the elementary school years are accompanied by predicted changes in intelligence and achievement test performance.

The situation regarding the effects of school anxiety on academic achievement is shown in Table 10. Generally, school anxiety has substantial relationships with academic achievement, except among Black children. Also, where school anxiety tends to have lower relations with teacher and peer appraisals, it also tends to have lower relations with school achievement, and vice versa. The two exceptions to this are for MC Anglo boys and Mexican-American girls. Overall, there are generally higher relations between school anxiety and school achievement than between school anxiety and teacher and peer appraisals. In support of this, there are 16 significant correlations involving school achievement, and only 11 involving teacher and peer appraisals. In relation to school problem behavior, while school anxiety is highly related to objective test performance among Mexican-Americans, in this subgroup it is unrelated to problem behaviors. Similarly, among ULC Anglo boys, school anxiety also is highly related to objective test performance, but it is not especially related to problem behaviors. Generalizing further, school anxiety appears to have more debilitating effects on academic achievement than it has on school problem behavior.

School Anxiety and Under- and Overachievement

Numerous researchers, both in psychology and in education, have for many years concerned themselves with the correlates of under- and overachievement. This is indicated, for example, by Taylor's (1964) review of the literature from 1933 to 1963. In addition, investigators have used various psychometric instruments and multivariate prediction techniques to increase the accuracy of predic-

Table 10 Correlations between School Anxiety and Academic Achievement, Intelligence

Variable	MC Anglo		ULC Anglo		Mexican-American		Black	
	Boys (N = 76)	Girls (N = 76)	Boys (N = 47)	Girls (N = 55)	Boys (N = 63)	Girls (N = 67)	Boys (N = 43)	Girls (N = 41)
MAT NV	−19	−20	−45†	−22	−36†	−33†		−26
MAT V	−12	−23*	−42†	−24	−33†	−44†	−29*	
CTMM NV	−24*	−23*	−20	−13	−40†	−35†	−21	−15
CTMM V	−19	−18	−32†	−27*	−36†	−34*	−11	

* Significant at .05 level
† Significant at .01 level
NOTE: Correlations less than .10, and decimals omitted

tions of scholastic achievement. Although they have been carried out separately, these two areas of research are in reality concerned with the same phenomena (Thorndike, 1963). Investigators in both areas are concerned with the observed discrepancy between predicted achievement and actual or observed achievement. Researchers in the former area may call the observed discrepancy under- or overachievement, while those concerned with prediction may call it prediction error. Regardless of the label one attaches to the discrepancy, this lack of correspondence between predicted and observed achievement has been the subject of many investigations.

Although the majority of studies have been at the high school and college level, it is recognized that underachievement at these levels often has its origins at the elementary level (Shaw & McCuen, 1960). There is still not enough information, however, concerning personality differences between under- and overachievers in the elementary school, and the investigation of personality concomitants of underachievement among elementary school children with different racial-ethnic backgrounds is pursued in this section.

In particular, we are interested in the relation of school anxiety to underachievement. Ordinarily, anxiety is negatively related to teacher grades at the elementary and high school level. However, anxiety and intelligence are also negatively related, and this relationship is usually attributed to the debilitating effects of anxiety on test performance. But this leaves us with an important question: Does anxiety independently influence achievement, or is the influence of anxiety dependent on its influence on intelligence tests, with intelligence being the direct influence on achievement?

The answer to this question is provided in Table 11, which is from a study by R. A. Adams and Phillips (1968). The school anxiety scale significantly correlated in a nega-

**Table 11   Correlates of Under- and Overachievement
for Children Classified by Racial-Ethnic Status**

Variable	Correlations			
	MC Anglo (N = 152)	ULC Anglo (N = 100)	Mexican American (N = 131)	Black (N = 74)
School motivation	.43†	.51†	.39†	.33†
School anxiety	−.15*	−.18*	.10	−.11
Feelings of inferiority	−.01	−.17*	−.08	−.09
Neurotic symptoms (academic)	−.24†	−21*	−18*	−.16
Neurotic symptoms (social)	−.08	−.11	−.18*	−.14
Aggression with independence strivings	−.14*	−.26†	−.09	−.12
Active withdrawal	−.21†	−.29†	−.11	−.23*
Emotional disturbance with depression	.05	0.	−.08	.01
Self-enhancement through derogation of others	−.01	−.04	−.12	−.07
Diffuse hyperactivity	−.05	.03	−.02	−.15
Peer acceptance	.36†	.24†	.37†	.32†
Peer rejection	−.20*	−.22*	−.14*	−.02

* Significant at .05 level (one-tailed t test)
† Significant at .01 level (one-tailed t test)
NOTE: Ns for Neurotic symptoms (academic) and Diffuse hyperactiiy are MC
Anglo = 144, ULC Anglo = 91, Black = 74, and Mexican-American = 118.

tive direction with under- and overachievement (UOA) in
two of the four subgroups. This indicates that high-anxious
students also tend to be students who perform at a level
below that which would be predicted based on knowledge
of their academic ability, and assuming that their ability
already is depressed by the effects of anxiety makes this
finding even more significant.

Although not central to this point, school motivation correlated between .33 and .51 with UOA within the four major subgroups. Considering the fact that the effect of intelligence on grades has been removed, these correlations are unusually high and add support to the construct validity of the school motivation scale. Another positive and highly significant correlate of UOA is that of peer acceptance (range: .24–.37).

School Anxiety and Masculinity- Femininity

Masculinity-femininity (M-F) considerations appear to have special explanatory power in relation to two major anxiety findings. One is the higher anxiety scores of girls, which S. B. Sarason's group (1960) explains primarily in terms of the higher defensiveness associated with masculinity compared to femininity. The other is the variation of sex differences in anxiety across sociocultural groups, which might be attributable to M-F.

Some studies of anxiety and M-F have been reported, although Ruebush (1963) cites only three dealing directly with the relation of anxiety and appropriate sex typing in children. Kagan and Moss (1962) report that the failure of boys to adopt masculine behaviors between the ages of 3 and 10 was found to be predictive of high sex anxiety for these boys as adults, but for girls sex-role attitudes and interests were not highly related to adult sex anxiety. Also, they report that fear of physical harm in boys of this age range was associated with difficulties of identification, but this was not true of girls. Sutton-Smith and Rosenberg (1960) used a games-preference inventory to obtain M-F scores for children in grades 4–6, and the CMAS to obtain anxiety scores. High-anxious boys' games choices were found to be more feminine and immature than those of low-anxious boys, but high- and low-anxious girls did not differ on the M-F aspects of their game preferences.

In a study by Gotts and Phillips (1968), 60 girls and 57 boys from fifth-grade classrooms in five racially and ethnically diverse schools served as subjects. The selection of racially-ethnically differentiated schools was mandated by the frequent reference throughout the literature to differential emphases on masculine-feminine sex typing in different subcultures (Kagan, 1964; Witkin, Dyk, Faterson, Goodenough, & Karp, 1962, Ch. 13). Social, racial, and ethnic characteristics of the five-school sample may be described as follows: (1) predominantly lower-class Black, (2) predominantly lower-class Mexican-American, (3) middle-class Anglo, (4) upper-lower-class Anglo, and (5) well-mixed Black, Mexican-American, and Anglo. Classrooms were of nearly identical size, so they could potentially make equal contributions to the definition of M-F norms.

Correlation coefficients were computed for boys and girls separately between M-F and intelligence scores (CTMM). Coefficients of -.12 were found for nonlanguage IQ for both sexes. Language IQ and M-F were related -.01 for boys and -.03 for girls. All of these findings were nonsignificant. It was concluded that the PPT M-F scores were uncontaminated by general intelligence.

The major hypothesis was tested by computing correlation coefficients between M-F and anxiety scores separately for boys and girls, and on the basis of the results of Table 12, a highly significant relation was found between M-F and anxiety for boys, while these variables were unrelated for girls. This result may be related to a further analysis of school behavioral correlates of M-F in boys and girls, and these additional results from the Gotts and Phillips (1968) study are reported in Table 13. For the Leary-Coffey (1955) dimensions the word underlined (Table 13) represents, in each instance, the numerically larger end of the bipolar pair (for determining the meaning of a correlation's direction), and a low M-F score is more masculine for boys and less feminine for girls (and conversely).

From the results, we see that more masculine boys are more blunt, distrustful, skeptical, activated, aggressive, competitive, exploitive, and managerial. Since these school behavior dimensions are based on teachers' observations, and the foregoing are characteristics that are generally more masculine, these results serve as a teacher-observational validation of the M-F scale, as well as supporting the significance of M-F in the anxiety of boys.

Table 12 Correlations between School Anxiety and M-F for Boys and Girls

Type of M-F scores	Boys	Girls
M-F (raw)	.44*	−.04
M-F (T)	.40*	−.06

* Significant at .01 level
NOTE: Boys, df = 56; Girls, df = 59

Table 13 Correlations between M-F and Dimensions of Problem Behavior

Dimensions	Boys (N = 48)	Girls (N = 53)
Blunt—Overconventional	−.46	NS
Responsible—Distrustful	.34	NS
Overgenerous—Skeptical	.40	NS
Activated—Quiescent	−.30	NS
Aggressive—Cooperative	−.43	NS
Competitive—Dependent	−.38	NS
Exploitive—Docile	−.44	NS
Managerial—Self-effacing	−.30	NS

NOTE: For all r's listed, $P < .05$ (two-tailed tests), and NS = nonsignificant.

SCHOOL ANXIETY AND POPULAR AND DISLIKED PEER CHOICES

Schachter (1959) has theorized that firstborn children experience more inconsistent nurturing from their parents than later-born children, and as a result show more dependency behavior. In a follow-up study, Schachter (1964) contended, granting that firstborn are more dependent and easily influenced, that in a sociometric situation, firstborn children will evaluate their friends more in terms of what others think of them than will later-born children. Using positive sociometric nominations, he found that firstborn subjects assigned more of their choices to persons who were popular among their peers than did later-born subjects.

Research on anxiety also has been concerned with dependency like behaviors. For example, Sarason and his co-workers (1960), in their theoretic consideration of the dynamics of test anxiety, stress the significance of dependency needs and behaviors. Furthermore, a number of studies have demonstrated specific relations between anxiety and dependency behaviors (I. G. Sarason, 1958; Walters & Karal, 1960), in several instances with school-age subjects.

Relying on results like those mentioned above, and the rationale behind them, Adams and Phillips investigated the relationship of anxiety to sociometric choice in an unpublished study (1966). It was anticipated that high-anxious children would have a greater tendency to choose popular peers and reject disliked peers than low-anxious children.

Arriving at an adequate measure of a child's "tendency to pick popular peers" and another measure of his "tendency to reject disliked peers" initially was intriguing, as well as difficult. After considerable thought it became clear that the peer nomination data offered an adequate as well as convenient means of obtaining the desired information.

With this information, a peer-acceptance (popularity) score and a peer-rejection (disliked) score were computed for each of 404 fourth-grade children by adding the popularity indexes for the five (or less) peers they chose positively on the sociometric instrument and dividing this figure by the number of persons chosen. An index of a child's tendency to reject disliked peers was similarly obtained.

Results Obtained

In the analyses presented in Table 14, which are reported in the study referred to above, the 202 children with the highest school anxiety scores were defined as the high-anxiety group, and the remaining 202 were defined as the low-anxiety group. An "F" test of significance, with respect to the tendency of these two groups to pick popular peers, showed a highly significant difference between these two groups in the predicted direction.

Although the tendency of high-anxious children to reject disliked peers more than low-anxious subjects is not as pronounced, the difference is significant and in the predicted direction. In addition, these tendencies of high-anxious children to pick popular peers and reject disliked peers more than low-anxious children, apply as well to the two sex groups considered separately.

Table 14   Mean Tendency to Pick Popular Peers and to Reject Disliked Peers for Children Classified by Anxiety

Subgroups compared	Mean tendency to pick popular peers	Mean tendency to reject disliked peers
High anxiety	.79	1.22
Low anxiety	.50	1.06
	$(P < .001)$	$(P = .04)$

SEX AND RACIAL- ETHNIC DIFFERENCES IN SCHOOL ANXIETY

Sex differences in anxiety, measured by questionnaire or self-report, have been consistently obtained, with girls usually having higher scores (Ruebush, 1963). This holds for test anxiety (e.g., Forbes, 1969; S. B. Sarason et al., 1960) and for general anxiety (Castenada, McCandless, & Palermo, 1956; Phillips, 1962). Actually, sex differences are the rule in psychologic research (Maccoby, 1966), although a recent report takes issue with this statement (Maccoby & Jacklin, 1975).

Sarason and his colleagues (1960) have dealt with sex differences at some length, and they tend to favor two correlated explanations of such differences. One is that boys are more defensive than girls primarily because it is easier for girls in American society to admit to anxiety. The admission of anxiety is less threatening to a girl's femininity than a boy's masculinity, and the anxious girl receives a more supportive response than the anxious boy. The other explanation is that the content of most anxiety scales taps areas of less concern to boys than girls.

However, the former explanation is most frequently given. In support of it, boys usually have higher defensiveness scores, i.e., they are less likely to admit common feelings, faults, etc. (e.g., K. Hill, 1963; Lighthall, 1963). This hypothesis also receives support from results with projective measures of anxiety (Phillips, 1966c), and in terms of conflict theory (Phillips, 1966b)

Some of the most significant influences in schools are those associated with social class and racial-ethnic status. One such finding is that LC, *minority*-status children consistently have higher levels of anxiety than other LC children (Phillips, 1966a; Tseng & Thompson, 1969). Reports also show LC children to be more anxious than MC children (Dunn, 1968; Hawkes & Koff, 1969).

Table 15   Summary of Analyses of Variance, with Sex
and Racial-Ethnic Status as Fixed Effects, and the
Factors of the School Anxiety Scale as Dependent
Variables

Factor		Means for all effects		P
1: Negative Valuation	A	1.78	2.50	.001
	B	1.78	2.49	.001
	A X B	1.46	2.10	.717
		2.11	2.89	
2: Taking Tests	A	2.34	3.71	.001
	B	2.67	3.39	.001
	A X B	2.18	2.51	.039
		3.17	4.26	
3: Lack of Confidence in	A	1.73	2.76	.001
Meeting Expectations of	B	2.23	2.26	.842
Others	A X B	1.88	1.57	.042
		2.58	2.95	
4: Physiologic Reactivity	A	0.94	1.86	.001
	B	1.06	1.74	.001
	A X B	.084	1.04	.002
		1.28	2.45	

NOTE: A =   Racial-Ethnic Status, with first means being for whites
         B =   Sex, with first means being for boys
      A X B =   Racial-Ethnic Status by sex, with columns being for sex (boys then
      girls), and rows being for Racial-Ethnic Status (Anglo, then Non-Anglo)

Whether these results apply to school anxiety is shown
in Table 15, which is based on data using the short form
of the SAS, and the results obtained are in general agree-
ment with what is usually reported. Boys achieve lower
scores than girls, except for Factor 3, Lack of Confidence
in Meeting Expectations of Others. This would mean, assuming boys are more defensive, that they actually are *more*

anxious in relation to meeting expectations of others. Considering the content of the items, this factor may reflect boys' concerns with *how they perceive themselves,* in contrast to the content of Factor 1, which may reflect girls' concerns with *how others perceive them.* Since girls tend to be more concerned with social relationships and what others think of them, the direction of differences between Factors 1 and 3 reinforces the notion that the content of areas tapped in anxiety scales contributes to sex differences. Further, it is likely that the content of a school anxiety scale would generally be more central to the concerns of girls than boys, since the elementary school is perceived by boys and girls as feminine (Kagan, 1964).

The other variable, racial-ethnic status, is usually confounded with social class. A Black or Mexican-American sample usually will be predominantly lower class, and it would have been difficult to match social class levels *across* racial-ethnic groups. Nonetheless, there are significant racial-ethnic differences on all the anxiety factors in Table 15, although whether racial-ethnic status is the factor actually involved is not determinable. The interaction effects, however, are more intelligible. Sex and racial-ethnic status interact to produce larger differences between boys and girls among Black and Mexican-American children than among Anglo children on Factor 2, Taking Tests, and Factor 4, Physiologic Reactivity. On Factor 1 there is no significant interaction, and for Factor 3 sex differences are reversed: Among Anglo children, boys are more anxious, but among Blacks and Mexican-Americans, girls are more anxious than boys.

ANTECEDENTS OF SOCIAL CLASS AND RACIAL-ETHNIC DIFFERENCES IN ANXIETY

Some insight into the etiology of social class and racial-ethnic differences in anxiety is offered in studies of defense and coping style. Some years ago Miller and Swanson (1960) reported that LC children utilized more primitive defenses (e.g., regression, denial) than MC children. More recently, in a longitudinal study of adolescents Weinstock (1967) found that childhood social class was negatively related to primitive mechanisms (e.g., denial), and positively related to the more mature defenses (e.g., projection, intellectualization), in support of the Miller and Swanson findings. Added to this, Miller and Swanson, as well as Weinstock, successfully related defense preference and style to the early family environment. For example, in Weinstock's research, denial, repression, regression, and displacement of aggression were all highly related to early parent-child relations, although the specific relationships often are complex.

A more direct relationship between anxiety and family environment also has been noted. S. B. Sarason et al. (1960) systematically explored differences between high- and low-test-anxious children's families within a psychoanalytic framework, and found a number of differences (especially involving mothers) in parental handling of evaluative situations. Adams and Sarason (1963) also found that children's anxiety was generally more related to their mother's than their father's anxiety.

In other studies, relations between anxiety and perceptions of parents have been investigated. Schultz, Firetto, & Walker (1969), for example, found a negative correlation between anxiety and the child's perception of his parents. In addition, in a study of adolescents (Phillips, Hindsman, & Jennings, 1960) it was found that anxiety was positively related to a pervasive dissatisfaction with others, including parents.

With specific reference to disadvantaged children, one of the critical findings, for our purposes, is that the parents of disadvantaged children provide less communication (Maas, 1951), and tend to have different approaches to discipline, relying more on external control as opposed to causal thinking and internal control (Kohn, 1959; Kohn & Carroll, 1960). This produces a deficit when entering school, where communication and internal controls are highly valued, and this may provide one causal factor in the development of anxiety in school.

Finally, it should be noted that general beliefs about the environment appear to be important etiologic factors in the higher levels of anxiety of LC, minority children. Katz (1968) has noted that ". . . debilitating anxiety in minority-group students may be more a function of perceived isolation and exclusion from the main American opportunity structure than awareness of one's intellectual limitations [p. 65]." In this connection, Schachter (1959) has postulated that social isolation produces anxiety, and one of the consequences of experiencing an anxiety-producing situation is a heightened tendency to seek affiliative relationships. If Katz is right, minority children have been put in double jeopardy—they not only are isolated and excluded from many school activities, which produces anxiety, but they are cut off from a major avenue for relieving anxiety in these circumstances, i.e., the opportunity for affiliative relations with significant others.

SCHOOL ANXIETY IN A CROSS-NATIONAL CONTEXT

This research focused on cross-cultural aspects of school anxiety in which children in three cultural subgroups, including Indian (Punjab state), Malay, and Chinese (Malaysian), were studied.[2] For comparative purposes, reference is also made to similar research in the United States, Yugoslavia, Australia, and Japan. The primary emphasis was on sex, socioeconomic status (SES), and age as factors related to school anxiety and its different dimensions. The extent of agreement/disagreement between findings was determined and the cross-cultural significance of such results was pursued. The study was carried out under the same conditions and involved the same samples, etc. as the study reported in Chapter 2.

Table 16 reports the anxiety means and standard deviations for each of the samples by sex and SES. Significant main and interaction effects for these variables, as well as for age, are reported in the discussion that follows. The probabilities associated with significant differences are also reported.

Culture

In the Malaysian sample Chinese subjects obtained higher scores than Malay subjects (2.4 vs. 2.1) on anxiety variable 4 ($p<.02$). They appear, therefore, to experience more physiologic stress than Malays. In addition, Indian (Punjab state) subjects consistently had lower anxiety scores, with the exception of test anxiety, than either Malay or Chinese (Malaysian) subjects.

Sex

Significant main effects for sex were found in the Malaysian sample on anxiety variables No. 2 and 5, and the sex effect on No. 1 approached significance. Females obtained higher test anxiety (females = 4.6, males = 4.1; $p<.001$), and higher total anxiety (females = 14.0, males = 13.3; $p<.01$). Either females experience more test anxiety and total anxiety, or they can at least express it more easily. The results for Rejection by Others (No. 1) were in the same direction, but were not significant ($p<.07$).

In the Indian sample, sex had a significant main effect on anxiety variables 1 (Rejection by Others), 4 (Physiologic Reactivity), and 5 (Total Anxiety). In all cases, females expressed more anxiety than males, their means being 2.9,

Table 16 Anxiety Means (Top) and SDs (Bottom) for Indian and Malaysian Subgroups

Anxiety variables	Indian				Malaysian — Malay				Malaysian — Chinese			
	High SES		Low SES		High SES		Low SES		High SES		Low SES	
	M $N=194$	F $N=126$	M $N=229$	F $N=144$	M $N=70$	F $N=76$	M $N=124$	F $N=127$	M $N=44$	F $N=40$	M $N=72$	F $N=48$
(1) Rejection by Others	2.4	2.7	2.8	3.0	3.8	4.0	3.6	4.0	3.9	3.8	3.4	3.9
	1.6	1.4	1.5	1.5	1.5	1.4	1.4	1.3	1.6	1.4	1.6	1.3
(2) Test Taking	4.1	4.1	4.3	4.6	3.8	4.7	4.3	4.3	4.0	4.5	4.2	4.8
	1.6	1.5	1.5	1.4	1.5	1.2	1.2	1.3	1.2	1.3	1.4	1.3
(3) Meeting Expectations of Others	1.8	2.1	2.1	2.0	3.4	3.4	3.4	3.3	3.3	3.2	3.2	3.4
	1.3	1.1	1.3	1.2	1.5	1.5	1.4	1.5	1.4	1.6	1.2	1.4
(4) Stress Reactivity	1.4	1.8	1.8	2.2	2.2	2.3	2.1	1.9	2.0	2.6	2.8	2.6
(5) Total Anxiety	9.7	10.7	11.0	11.8	13.2	14.4	13.4	13.5	13.2	14.1	13.6	14.7
	4.7	3.6	4.4	4.1	4.2	3.7	3.7	3.6	3.9	4.2	5.3	3.8

(No. 1), 2.0 (No. 4), and 11.2 (No. 5), in contrast to 2.6, 1.6, and 10.4, respectively, for males. The probabilities for these results were: $p<.016$ on No. 1, $p<.002$ (No. 4), and $p<.008$ (No. 5). Females also had higher scores on the other anxiety variables, but they lacked significance, as did all the interactions involving sex.

Age

In the Malaysian sample, significant age effects were obtained on anxiety variables No. 1, 4, and 5. For Rejection by Others, scores increased from age 9 through 12 (p $<.001$). This would be expected if children in this age range are progressively more peer-dominated and, consequently, more dependent on peer acceptance. A different pattern was found for physiologic reactivity, where scores increased from age 9 to 11 and then decreased at age 12 ($p<.03$), and the same trend was obtained for total anxiety ($p<.02$).

In the Indian sample, there were significant age effects on variables No. 2 ($p<.001$), 3 ($p<.002$), 4 ($p<.03$), and 5 ($p<.005$). In all cases, younger subjects had higher anxiety scores than older subjects. There also was a significant interaction involving SES on anxiety variable No. 4 (p $<.02$). Younger lower-SES subjects had higher physiologic reactivity than younger higher-SES subjects, but the reverse was true for older subjects. Overall, younger Malaysians were less anxious than older Malaysians, while the opposite was true of Indians.

To show the age trend more clearly, the total anxiety means at each age are given in Table 17.

Although the age ranges of the two samples do not coincide, anxiety increases until age 11, and then declines through age 13, followed by a large increase at age 14, and then another decline. At age 16, anxiety is lower than at any other age. Overall, no clear pattern emerges, and whether

Table 17   Total Anxiety Means and SDs at Each Age
for Malaysians and Indians

Sample	Age							
	9	10	11	12	13	14	15	16
Malaysian								
Mean	12.6	13.8	14.2	13.5				
SD	4.0	4.2	3.7	3.8				
N	97	165	186	138				
Indian								
Mean		10.6	12.1	10.4	9.4	11.3	11.2	9.0
SD		3.1	3.9	4.4	3.4	4.1	3.8	4.0
N		126	144	96	101	101	56	69

this is due to sampling variability, or to the lack of an inherent age-relatedness, cannot be ascertained.[3]

Socioeconomic Status

In the Malaysian sample, there were no significant main effects for SES, although there was an interaction between SES and race on anxiety variables No. 4 ($p < .03$) and 5 ($p < .05$). Upper-SES Malays obtained higher anxiety scores than lower-SES Malays, but for the Chinese Malaysians this pattern was reversed.

In the Indian sample, SES significantly affected anxiety variables No. 1, 2, 4, and 5. In all cases lower-SES subjects had the higher anxiety scores, the probabilities for these differences being: Rejection by Others, $p < .01$; Taking Tests, $p < .004$; Physiologic Reactivity, $p < .002$; and Total Anxiety, $p < .002$.

In summary, clear and expected SES differences occurred only among Indians. Among the Malaysians, SES differences were masked by SES by culture interactions.

Summary and Discussion

This attempt to find out if sex, SES, and age affects the school anxiety of Malaysian and Indian children was stimulated and guided by previous research in the United States. On the basis of this research it was expected that sex and socioeconomic status definitely would affect the anxiety of these children, but an expectation regarding age was not justified by the available literature.

With regard to age, significant age differences in school anxiety occurred. But the age trends were unreliable and difficult to interpret. However, on the average, younger Malaysians were less school-anxious than their older counterparts, while among Indians the opposite was true. In Nijhawan's study (1972), which included Indian subjects 11–14 years old, age differences did not occur on the TASC. In contrast, Hill and Sarason (1966) report that text anxiety increases from grade 1 to grade 6. In addition, an age x SES interaction occurred in our Indian sample which was not observed by Nijhawan. In substance, while there are age differences in school anxiety, these do not appear to be age-related in any consistent pattern.

Sex made a generally significant contribution to school anxiety, although there were no significant interactions involving sex. As expected, girls had higher anxiety scores than boys, and similar sex differences using the same school anxiety scale also have been reported for Yugoslavian (Phillips, Martin, & Zorman, 1971), Australian,[4] and Japanese[5] children. In addition, Ng (1971) also found similar, but nonsignificant, sex differences using several different anxiety instruments. This uniformity of results could mean that sex differences in school anxiety are largely independent of cultural influences; or it might indicate that sex socialization practices, as they relate to the development of school anxiety, are uniform across these particular cultures. In addition, these results could be interpreted to mean that girls are more school-anxious, or are more willing to admit anxiety.

Clear SES differences were obtained in the Indian sample, which confirms the findings of Nijhawan (1972), who reports that lower-SES children were more anxious, using the TASC and GASC, although she had expected opposite results. They also are consistent with results for Yugoslavian (Phillips et al., 1971) and Australian[4] children. Socioeconomic results for the Malaysians, however, were dependent on race, and opposite findings occurred for Malay and Chinese (Malaysian) children. Results for the Chinese were like those for the Indian subjects (and, it might be added, like those obtained in American studies), but upper-SES Malay children obtained higher scores than their lower-SES counterparts.

These latter deviant results could be interpreted in terms of schooling arrangements. Malay children go either to Malay-language schools or to schools taught in English, while Chinese children usually attend English medium schools. This means that Malay children are considerably more segregated socioeconomically, with lower-SES Malaysians attending Malay medium schools and higher-SES Malays attending English medium schools. In contrast, both higher- and lower-SES Chinese tend to go to the same schools. Lower-SES Chinese, therefore, are in direct competition with higher-SES Chinese in school, and it is understandable that they would be more school-anxious. In contrast, lower-SES Malays are in competition with themselves, rather than with higher-SES Malays, who are competing with Chinese students in the English medium classes. In such circumstances it is not surprising that they are more school-anxious than lower-SES Malays. This view receives indirect support from the Nijhawan study, where it was found that in rural areas, upper-class children in private schools had higher TASC scores than upper-class children attending government schools. In urban areas, on the other hand, lower-class children attending government schools had higher TASC scores than lower-class children in private schools. Nevertheless, the situation is probably complex and not conducive to simple explanations; and it should be further noted that, as a group, Malays were on the average no more school-anxious than the Chinese.

In conclusion, the results taken as a whole indicate that there is a substantial degree of intercultural generality in at least certain aspects of school anxiety. But having identified such cultural invariance, there is still the difficult task of accounting for it.

NOTES

1. Some portions of this chapter are based on an earlier analysis of interventions in relation to anxiety in school by Phillips, Martin, and Meyers (1972).

2. This study was conducted in cooperation with Shyam L. Ahuja, a native of India, who returned to India for the purpose of this study, Norman Charles Harris; and Ng See Ngean, a Professor at the University of Malaya, who carried out that part of the study.

3. As a further indication of this instability, data obtained from Professor Iwawaki (Footnote 5 below) show the following age-grade means: 9 yrs (3rd) = 11.9, 10 yrs (4th) = 11.0, 11 yrs (5th) = 10.6, and 12 yrs (6th) = 11.4.

4. Data based on Short-Form of the CSQ obtained through personal communication with Professor Terence A. Heys, Sydney Teachers College, Newton, N. S. W., Australia.

5. Data based on Short-Form of the CSQ obtained through personal communication with Professor Saburo Iwawaki, Department of Psychology, Chukyo University, Nagoya, Japan.

Chapter 4

SPECIAL STUDIES OF EFFECTS OF SCHOOLING ON ANXIETY

In this chapter we report on a number of special studies, including one on school environmental effects on anxiety, and a discussion of the affective significance of the school environment in different subcultures. There also are studies of the relation of early school experience to the development of school anxiety, and a discussion of the effects of graded vs. nongraded programs on school anxiety. The chapter ends with an analysis of the role of anxiety and related factors in an integrated elementary school environment.

THE SCHOOL VS. OUT-OF- SCHOOL PARADIGM FOR ANALYZING THE INFLUENCE OF THE SCHOOL ENVIRONMENT

It has been popular and necessary to try to assess the contribution of the school environment to the school deficiencies of Blacks and other low-income minorities. In the

Coleman study (Coleman, Campbell, Hobson, McPartland, Mood, Weinfeld, & York 1966) it was concluded that most of the differences between children in school achievement are differences *within* rather than *between* schools. This suggests that factors like socioeconomic status and attitudes toward school are of crucial importance. Although the influence of the school environment thus appears to be small, they did find that its effects were greater on Blacks and other low-income minorities. The authors recognize the tenuousness of these generalizations, however, and appreciate the limitations of cross-sectional data in demonstrating a school environmental influence. In addition, in the Coleman study, as well as other studies of the influence of the school environment, the effects of the out-of-school environment were separated from the effects of the in-school environment by statistically controlling out-of-school environmental factors.

An alternative approach is to try to determine whether being in the school environment is associated with systematic *changes* in school behavior, using a rationale that rests upon the assumption that school behavior is influenced by maturational, out-of-school environmental, and school environmental factors. Children are generally in school about 9 months of the year, and are usually out of school the other 3 months. Thus a natural quasiexperimental design exists which has potential for separating the effects of the school environment from other effects.

This paradigm requires measures of school behavior at the beginning and end of the school year over a period of 2 or more years. By analyzing the trend in these school behavior variables during the school year in comparison with the trend during the summer months, the effects of the school environment (if present) presumably can be discerned. In utilizing this model, two further assumptions are made: That the effects of maturation are not systematically different for the school year and the summer months; and that children attend school in insignificant numbers during the summer months.

In this quasiexperimental paradigm, measurements of variables are obtained at the beginning and end of each school year, as shown in Figure 6, and the trend in the measurements between T_1 and T_2, T_2 and T_3, and T_3 and T_4 is determined. In the usual experimental and quasiexperimental design, one introduces a variable or treatment into the situation, and then sees what happens. In this instance we take something out, i.e., the children. If the trend of measurements on the variable changes when we take the children out of the school environment, and again when we put them back, then we suppose that the variable is significantly influenced by the school environment, provided that alternative or rival hypotheses can be ruled out. Examining the nature of the shifts under these conditions makes it possible to draw inferences about the direction of the influence. Some possible outcomes of results are shown in Figure 6.

One would be unjustified in inferring that the school environment had an effect if the results shown in A and E were obtained, since changes in A are uniform across the three periods of time, and in E there are no changes in the variable. In B, C, and D, however, an inference can be tentatively made that the school environment has a different effect than the out-of-school environment, provided that other interpretations are not more (or equally) plausible. In B we could conclude that the out-of-school environment decreases the variable, while the school environment increases it. In C we could say that the out-of- school environment has no effect, while the school environment increases the variable. And in D it appears that the school environment strongly decreases the variable and the out-of-school environment strongly increases it.

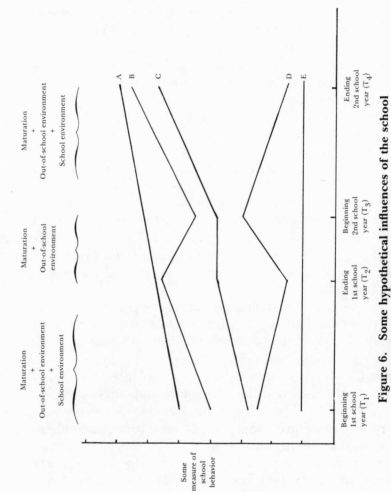

Figure 6. Some hypothetical influences of the school and out-of-school environment paradigm

The Paradigm Applied to School Anxiety

If the school environment becomes increasingly stressful, school anxiety should increase during the school year, but remain stable or return to a lower level by the beginning of the next school year. A summary of the repeated-measures analyses of variance is presented in Table 18.

There is a significant trials effect for school anxiety ($T_1 = 33.8, T_2 = 30.4, T_3 = 26.7, T_4 = 26.0$), but there is a steady erosion of scores. However, the largest difference occurs across the summer months. There also is a significant Racial-Ethnic Status X Trials interaction, and these means are found in Table 19. Generally, there are decreas-

Table 18 Summary of Repeated Measures Analyses of Variance of School Anxiety Variable

Source of within subjects' variance	df	F ratio	P
T	3,1029	40.0	$<.001$
A x T	9,1029	2.3	.015
B x T	3,1029	3.3	.020
A x B x T	9,1029	1.3	.207

NOTE: T = Trials; A = racial-Ethnic Status; B = Sex

Table 19 Mean School Anxiety Scores for Racial-Ethnic Subgroups on Different Trials

Subgroup	T_1	T_2	T_3	T_4
MC Anglo	23.1	22.1	18.7	20.4
ULC Anglo	30.4	26.6	21.5	22.4
Mexican-American	37.5	34.5	30.0	29.1
Black	44.4	38.4	36.6	32.2

NOTE: T_1 = Beginning of 4th grade T_2 = End of 4th grade
      T_3 = Beginning of 5th grade T_4 = End of 5th grade

**Table 20   Mean School Anxiety Scores for Sex
Subgroups on Different Trials**

Subgroup	T_1	T_2	T_3	T_4
Boys	29.8	28.8	24.6	23.6
Girls	37.9	32.0	28.8	28.4

NOTE: T_1 = Beginning of 4th grade T_2 = End of 4th grade
T_3 = Beginning of 5th grade T_4 = End of 5th grade

ing differences between subgroups from T_1 to T_4, primarily
because of the greater changes among the non-Anglo children, especially the Blacks. There actually are *increases* in
school anxiety during fifth grade among Anglo children.
Finally, there is a significant Sex X Trials interaction, with
these means listed in Table 20. One aspect of this sex
difference is the much larger decrease in school anxiety
during fourth grade among girls than boys.

If boys are less willing to admit to anxiety, then why do
girls show a larger decrease in anxiety scores than boys?
Perhaps girls are initially less defensive, but repeated testing increases their defensive mobilization more than it does
that of boys. Another possibility is that girls obtain higher
anxiety scores initially because they are more acquiescent
(and acquiescence is reactive to repeated testing).

The overall changes in anxiety across fourth and fifth
grade may be reflections of developmental (age) and
school changes. There is some evidence that anxiety
reaches a peak in the elementary school years at about 10
years of age, when most children are in fourth grade, and
this could be an important source of the decline in scores
from the beginning of the fourth grade.

The data presented in Figure 7 supply additional information on this possibility. A boy and a girl at each grade
level (grades 1–6) in each of the 15 elementary schools
eligible for Title 1 funds in the community were

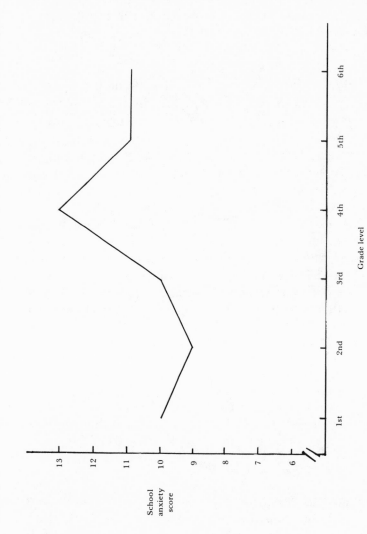

Figure 7. *Median School Anxiety* scores of children in 15 elementary schools

Grade level

School anxiety score

selected on a strictly random basis. These children were individually administered a short form of the *School Anxiety Scale* near the end of the school year by the counselors in these schools, with every effort being made to ensure that the children understood the items and responded under as relaxed conditions as possible.

Although based on small samples of children at each grade level, school anxiety is generally higher in the intermediate grades (grades 4–6) than in the primary grades (grades 1–3). In addition, the main increase in anxiety occurs between third and fourth grade, and there is a decline in anxiety between fourth and fifth grade, just as was obtained in the data already discussed.

There is some logical basis for expecting this increase between third and fourth grade, since the developmental changes of the children themselves may add to school pressures. In addition, there appears to be a shift in the philosophy of schooling at that point, to a more subject-centered, age-graded, and academic curriculum. Teachers in the primary grades also are somewhat more progressive in their teaching strategies and aims.

Overall, the data are suggestive of a school environmental effect, but the lack of controls for possible repeated-testing effects on school anxiety scores, and the uncertain effects of other factors, make a firm generalization risky.

INFLUENCE OF SCHOOL ENVIRONMENT ON AFFECTIVE MEANING

The semantic differential type scale has been widely used to measure meaning, and the generality of the dimensions of evaluation, potency, and activity has been suggested in a wide range of analyses. As to the nature of the meaning being measured, Miron and Osgood (1966) propose that the semantic differential measures qualitative meaning in the affective domain. They further state that the three dimensions reflect basic reponses on an affective level to the environment. Or, to put it the way Miron and Osgood (1966) do, there are three aspects to the individual's primitive, basic interaction with his environment. One is satisfaction-dissatisfaction, which is induced through these interactions; the evaluative factor is a measure of this interaction. Another is the amount of effort or work these interactions demand of the individual; the potency factor is a measure of this interaction. The third is the degree to which these interactions arouse the individual; this is measured by the activity factor. The conclusion that individuals share a common affective framework in no way implies that they also share common meanings for the concepts differentiated within this framework. In fact, there is considerable evidence that meanings for concepts vary both intra- and interculturally (Miron and Osgood, 1966).

In a study by McNeil and Phillips (1969), it was argued that racial-ethnic subgroups communicate and compete in the same general culture, and the extent to which the subcultures studied have succeeded in attaining the core culture (i.e., in being socialized) was hypothesized as follows, from most to least: MC Anglos, LC Anglos, Blacks, and Mexican-Americans. Mexican-Americans were hypothesized to be at the bottom of the socialization continuum because of the foreign language influence in many of their homes and also because of bicultural influences that make the Mexican-American's outlook different from that of the core culture (Rubel, 1966).

Concomitant with an increased level of socialization should be a change in an individual's view of his environment. This change should be evident in an individual's semantic connotative meaning, so that looking at an individual's semantic connotative meaning may provide information as to the level of his socialization. Thus, the more socialized a subcultural group is, the more closely that subcultural group's profile of semantic connotative meaning should resemble that of the core culture.

The major conclusions of the study appear in summary to indicate that the affective meaning of the total environment and the degree of socialization into the core culture are conditioned by school achievement and aptitude in all the subcultures. This occurs about equally in the MC Anglo and the non-Anglo subgroups, and to a somewhat greater degree in the ULC Anglo subgroups. However, within the MC Anglo subculture, affective meaning and core-culture socialization appear to be uninfluenced by other aspects of school experience, suggesting by implication that out-of-school experience is more determinant of the other antecedents of this basic response structure. Or, to put it into another context, for MC Anglos there appears to be only one discontinuity between their total environment and their school environment.

Within the ULC Anglo subculture, this basic response structure appears to be influenced by an additional dimension of school experience indicated by peer acceptance, emotional disturbance with depression, and school motivation. It appears that this dimension is related to dependency, conflict, and need for acceptance by self, peers, and teachers. In view of the nature of this dimension, it could possibly be described as a *concern with acceptance.* ULC families are identified with middle-class values, frequently aspire to upward mobility and middle-class status, and usually see the schools as the primary means towards this end. In addition, there is a middle-class orientation in the schools. It is not surprising, therefore, that concern with acceptance should represent an important discontinuity between their total environment and their school environment.

The basic response structure within the Black subculture appears to be influenced by a dimension of school experience indicated by emotional disturbance, active withdrawal, and feelings of inferiority. What is involved here seems to include dependency, conflict, passive coping with school environmental demands, and feelings of inferiority. Taken together, these variables point to an underlying dimension of passivity as part of the Black's basic affective and socialization pattern. Passivity, therefore, may represent an important discontinuity between their total environment and their school environment (in the Texas city studied).

Within the Mexican-American subculture, this basic response structure seems to be influenced by a dimension of school experience indicated by school anxiety, neurotic symptoms in social situations, and proneness toward neuroticism. These variables seem to involve general maladjustment and a pervasive hostility toward the school environment (and authority). "Alienation" may be the key element in this dimension, and the Mexican- American's life-style combined with the characteristics of schools serving Mexican-American neighborhoods, may form the basis of alienation (Rubel, 1966).

In summary, in all but the MC Anglo subculture this basic response structure is more influenced by at least one other school-related factor than it is by school achievement and aptitude. This may mean that the school environment is more an integral part of the total environment of the MC Anglo subculture, or it may mean that the family and peers are more important sources of influence on the basic response structure of the MC Anglo child. In view of the overall results, the negative affective meaning and lack of socialization into the core culture of minority children go beyond academic deficiencies and involve other dimensions of school experience. It also seems, by implication, that we have further support for the importance of affective education.

EARLY SCHOOL EXPERIENCE

The importance of early school stress is suggested by two prominent conceptions of anxiety. One is Sarason's (Sarason et al., 1960); he emphasizes the effects of negative evaluation in the preschool home, and then in the early school years. The other is Atkinson's theory of achievement motivation (Atkinson & Feather, 1966), where anxiety is related to the need to avoid failure, which is a disposition with origins in early experiences with achievement situations. Inadequate school socialization and the experiences of failure in the early grades, therefore, should be antecedent to school stress and anxiety reactions which are observed later.

Adequate school socialization involves adaptation to the social (interpersonal) and academic demands of schooling. Children must learn to participate on a continuing basis in highly structured group activities and to adapt to an adult whose relationships are conditioned by his teaching role. They must learn from instruction that is largely verbal and requires sustained periods of attention, prescribed work habits, and so forth. And they must relate to and compete with peers varying greatly in intellectual and other ways that are advantageous to some and disadvantageous to others. In consideration of these and other salient features of early school experiences, an important question should be raised: Which is more important in the development of stress and anxiety reactions in school—failure in meeting the social demands of school socialization, or failure in meeting the academic demands of school socialization? This question was tentatively answered in a study by Phillips (1967).

The design of the study involved the use of measures of success/failure in meeting the social and academic demands of schooling in grades 1–3 as predictors of stress and anxiety reactions in fourth grade. The predictors used were as follows:

(1) Success/failure in meeting social demands, including appropriate conduct (i.e., Es in conduct in first, second, and third grade); inappropriate conduct (i.e., Us and Xs in conduct in first, second, and third grade) (2) Success/failure in meeting both social and academic demands, including teacher grades (i.e., subject-matter grades in first, second, and third grade); basal reading level in first, second, and third grade (3) Success/failure in meeting academic demands, including objectively measured achievement (i.e., readiness test scores in first grade, and MAT, CTMM scores in second grade)

When we look at the results in Table 21, we find that subject-matter grades are generally predictive of anxiety, with the exception of non-Anglos. Basal reading level also correlates with anxiety, although there is an interesting sex difference. The correlations for boys increase across grades, reaching a high of –.38 in third grade, while the reverse trend occurs for girls, with the highest correlation (–.49) being in first grade.

Appropriate and inappropriate conduct follow this same trend. The correlations for appropriate conduct *increase* from first to third grade (reaching –.49) among boys, but not among girls. In contrast, correlations for inappropriate conduct *decrease* from first to third grade among girls only, starting with a high of .43 in first grade.

In summary, there are two important sex differences in these results. It is *low* basal reading level and *inappropriate* conduct that predict *higher* anxiety among girls; and it is *high* basal reading level and *appropriate* conduct that predict *lower* anxiety among boys. The other difference is that *first grade* low basal reading level and *inappropriate* conduct appear to raise the anxiety of girls, but not of boys.

These results may be related to the developmental lag of boys, sex-role and socialization differences, and the feminine orientation of elementary schools. Girls are ex-

**Table 21 Correlations of ± 20 or Higher between
School Experience (in Grades 1–3) and School Anxiety
in Fourth Grade**

Prior school experience	School anxiety			
variable	Boys	Girls	Anglo	Non-Anglo
1st grade				
Subject matter grades		−25		
Es in conduct	−27			−23
Us, Xs in conduct		43		22
Basal reading level		−49		−36
Readiness Test, Reading*		26		
Readiness Test, Numbers*	28	29		
2nd grade				
Subject matter grades	−25	−29	−23	
Es in conduct	−29			
Us, Xs in conduct				
Basal reading level	−32	−26	−21	
CTMM Language IQ	−34	−36	−21	
CTMM Non Language IQ	−25	−34	−21	
MAT, Reading	−24	−47	−22	−28
MAT, Arithmetic		−40	−20	
3rd grade				
Subject matter grades	−24	−29	−25	
Es in conduct	−49	−33	−31	−21
Us, Xs in conduct				
Basal reading level	−38	−28		−26

* Readiness test scores are inverse to degree of readiness.
NOTE: Decimal points are omitted.

pected to do well in school, and to do so does not add especially to the attention, security, satifaction, and self-confidence they obtain from school. At the same time, it may be more threatening for a girl to do poorly in school than it is for boys. In contrast, boys are not expected to do as well, so that when they do they may receive more attention from their teachers and peers than girls.

This is supported by an examination of objectively measured achievement. The *Metropolitan Readiness Test* in grade 1 and the MAT in grade 2 produced higher correlations with anxiety for girls than for boys. The differences are especially pronounced for the MAT.

EFFECTS OF A GRADED VS. A NONGRADED PROGRAM ON SCHOOL ANXIETY

One implication of the educational claims made for nongraded organization of children for instructional purposes is that children in such programs ought to be less school-anxious. In an unpublished study, Chandler (1969) summarizes these psychologic implications, and the following report presents the main outcomes of that investigation.

A nongraded group was initially established in a large and progressive, upper-middle-class elementary school with children who would otherwise have been designated as third-, fourth-, and fifth-graders. These children were randomly selected from the available pool of children, as were the children who made up the regular third-, fourth-, and fifth-grade control classes. The short form of the *School Anxiety Scale* was administered early in the school year in which this educational experiment began, and again early in the next 2 school years. The analyses to be reported concern only those experimental and control children who were third- and fourth-graders (or would be designated as such if they were not in the nongraded program) at the beginning of the study, and who had been in the experimental and control groups through the third year of testing, which was after 2 school years of experiences in the graded or nongraded programs.

Mean school anxiety scores for these children are shown in Figure 8. Because of a decided shift in the means between Trials 1 and 2 (i.e., during the first school year in

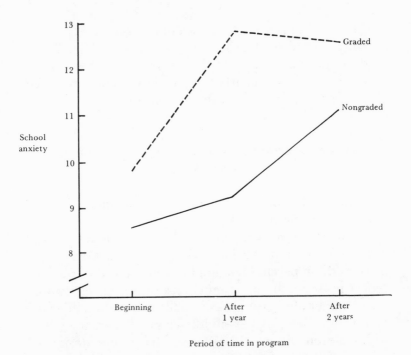

Figure 8. Means on *School Anxiety Scale* of graded
and nongraded groups at the beginning, after 1 year,
and after 2 years

the program) in comparison with the shift between Trials
2 and 3 (i.e., during the second year in the program), separate repeated measures analyses of variance were performed— one for Trials 1 and 2, and another for Trials 2
and 3. A summary of these analyses of variance is presented
in Table 22.

The results of the analyses show a highly significant
increase in school anxiety during the first year. Although
most of this increase seems to be due to the graded children, the interaction only approaches statistical significance. For the second year in the experiment only the main
effect of graded vs. nongraded organization approached
significance.

Table 22   Summary of Repeated Measures Analyses of Variance of the Effects of Graded vs. Nongraded Programs on School Anxiety

Period of time in program	Source of variance	df	F ratio	P
During first school year in the program, i.e., Trial 1 to Trial 2	Between Graded vs. Nongraded	1,89	3.1	.08
	Within Trials	1,89	9.5	.003
	Graded/ Nongraded x Trials	1,89	2.4	.12
During second school year in the program, i.e., Trial 2 to Trial 3	Between Graded/ Nongraded	1,89	3.0	.08
	Within Trials	1,89	0.5	.51
	Graded/ Nongraded x Trials	1,89	1.7	.19

In summary, the results for only the first year of the experiment are in the predicted direction. Both third- and fourth-graders in the nongraded groups remained at approximately the same level of anxiety during this year, while comparable children in the graded groups increased in anxiety. Then, a curious thing happened. Now the graded group stayed about the same in school anxiety, as did the fourth-graders (who were now in what is equivalent to fifth grade) in the nongraded group. But the third-graders in the nongraded group (who were now the equivalent of fourth-graders) increased drastically in school anxiety.

In exploring reasons for this shift, consideration was first given to the possibility of strong Hawthornelike effects during the first year of the experiment. This might have helped to account for the near-superiority of the non-graded children over the graded children in terms of changes in school anxiety. With the exception of the non-graded group who were the equivalent of third-graders in the first year, there were small changes in school anxiety during the second year, which one might expect as the Hawthorne effect dissipated.

However, additional information was obtained in another phase (D. H. Williams, 1968) of this experimental program. Williams utilized observational and interview techniques to ascertain the ways in which the nongraded and graded (control) programs actually differed. Using criteria relevant to the advantages of nongraded organizational patterns, he found that the nongraded group's experiences were generally indistinguishable from those of the graded group *after the first year.* This suggests that the reversal of results between the first and second year of the experiment may reflect a deterioration in the experiences that were supposed to have been provided, so that by the second year both the Hawthorne and treatment effects had dissipated. In conclusion, the results should serve to remind us of the difficulties of educational experimentation (Miles, 1964), and of the importance of knowledge of the adequacy/inadequacy of implementation of experimental as well as of control conditions.

SCHOOL ANXIETY IN AN INTEGRATED ELEMENTARY SCHOOL ENVIRONMENT

In the 1973–74 school year a large school district in the Southwest introduced an innovative approach to integration at the elementary school level. This was the Sixth-Grade Learning Center, to which all sixth-grade students, except the few living in the immediate area, were bused. The percentage of Anglos, Mexican-Americans, and Blacks was balanced so as to approximate the percentages of these racial-ethnic groups in the school population. The study reported here was planned to coincide with the beginning of this integration effort, so that data could be obtained at the beginning of the first full school year of operation, as well as at the end.

The purpose of the study was to describe the student population at one Sixth-Grade Learning Center in terms of prior elementary school attended, school anxiety, and a number of other sociopsychologic and educational variables. In addition, there was an effort to ascertain racial-ethnic subgroup differences on these variables, and to determine the extent and nature of the changes in these variables during the school year. There also was an effort to determine the predictability of achievement for different racial- ethnic subgroups, and a concern for the implications of such results for school academic learning in an integrated environment.

The specific focus of this report, however, is on school anxiety, although other aspects of the overall project are introduced where necessary. For a full report of the study the reader is referred to Schilhab (1976).

Racial-Ethnic and Sex Differences in School Anxiety During the School Year

The mean total school anxiety scores at the beginning and end of the school year are given for the Racial-Ethnic and Sex subgroups and the total sample in Table 23. An analysis of variance of these scores also was carried out, incorporating Sex as an additional "independent" variable.

The result for racial-ethnic status was insignificant, but there was a significant sex main effect ($F = 4.11$; df $= 1,634$; $p < .05$), with girls having higher scores. In addition, the difference between the pretest in October–November and the posttest in April–May was highly significant ($F = 32.26$; df $= 1,634$; $p < .01$), with total anxiety scores being *lower* at the end of the school year for the total sample.

Table 23   Mean Scores on Factors of School Anxiety*

	Anxiety factors			
Group	Fear of Rejection	Test Taking	Expectations of Others	Stress Reactivity
Anglos				
Period 1	3.8	3.4	2.4	2.1
Period 2	3.2	2.7	2.3	1.6
Blacks				
Period 1	2.6	3.9	2.9	2.2
Period 2	2.3	3.9	2.9	2.1
Mexican-Americans				
Period 1	3.7	3.8	3.0	2.4
Period 2	2.9	3.2	2.6	1.7
Males				
Period 1	3.1	3.5	2.8	2.2
Period 2	2.5	3.1	2.7	1.7
Females				
Period 1	3.6	3.8	2.7	2.3
Period 2	3.1	3.4	2.5	1.9
Total sample				
Period 1	3.5	3.5	2.6	2.2
Period 2	3.0	3.0	2.5	1.7

* Period 1: Fall (Oct.-Nov.) 1973
  Period 2: Spring (Apr.-May) 1974
NOTE: Taken from Schilhab (1976)

There also was a significant interaction effect involving Racial-Ethnic Status and Period of Testing ($F = 5.69$; df = 2,634; $p<.01$). To summarize this result, the lower school anxiety reported earlier for the total sample didn't apply to Black children.

In the context of integration, these results can be considered promising, since it is generally assumed that desegregation will be accompanied by increased stress and anxiety (among other things), with little hope that such tensions will quickly dissipate. This was not the case, however, in this newly integrated Sixth-Grade Learning Center, with the exception of Black children.

We now turn to results for the different dimensions of school anxiety, which are depicted in Figures 9 and 10. (The origin of these factorial dimensions was previously described in Chapter 2.) One notes that Anglos scored highest on the Fear of Rejection factor and Blacks had their highest scores on the Test-Taking factor, while Mexican-American students had high scores on both of these factors. In addition, males as a group had a pattern of scores similar to that shown by Black students, while females had a pattern similar to that of the Mexican-American group.

These results were examined further using analysis of variance techniques. Although girls had higher total school anxiety scores, only results for the Fear of Rejection factor were significant among the individual dimensions of school anxiety ($F = 6.78$; $df = 1,634$; $p < .01$). Racial-Ethnic Status differences were significant, however, for all but the Stress Reactivity factor. Blacks were especially low on the Fear of Rejection factor, while Anglos were low on the Test Taking and Expectations of Others factors.

The effects of time of testing were significant for all four factors, with anxiety being lower at the end of the year in all instances. But when interactions were examined, only one was significant. This occurred for the Test-Taking factor and involved Racial-Ethnic Status and Testing Period. On this factor, scores increased for Black students over the school year, but decreased for the other two racial-ethnic groups ($F = 3.03$; $df = 2,634$; $p < .05$).

School Anxiety as a Predictor of School Academic Learning

As previously noted, a major concern of the study was the extent to which we could predict school year-end achieve-

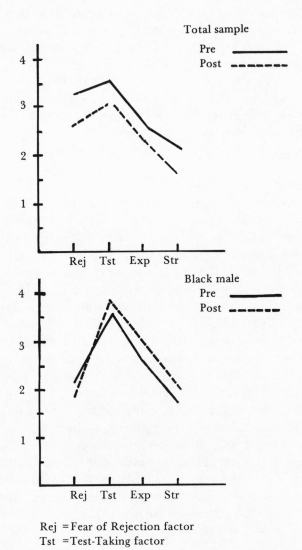

Rej = Fear of Rejection factor
Tst = Test-Taking factor

Figure 9. Mean scores on factors of school anxiety for total sample and male subgroups (from Schilhab, 1976)

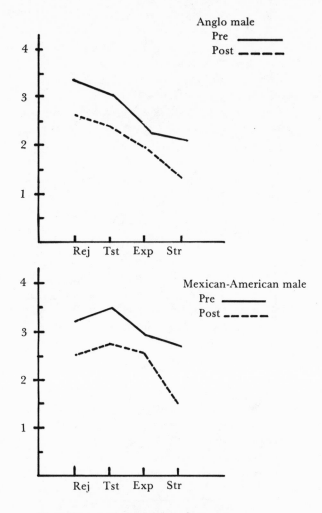

Exp = Expectation of Others factor
Str = Stress Reactivity factor

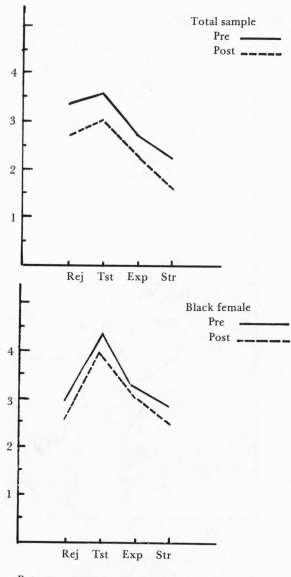

Rej = Fear of Rejection factor
Tst = Test-Taking factor

Figure 10. Mean scores on factors of school anxiety for total sample and female subgroups (from Schilhab, 1976)

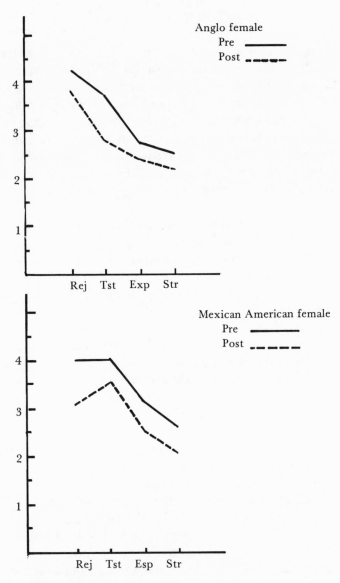

Exp = Expectation of Others factor
Str = Stress Reactivity factor

ment in reading and mathematics, using a regression model. This emphasis was of special interest because the nature of the statistical controls utilized allowed us to assess the contribution of school anxiety and other factors to school academic learning in an integrated setting.

A number of variables were included in the prediction models, and these are briefly summarized below. For a more complete description of these variables the reader should consult Schilhab (1976).

1. School Anxiety—utilized the short form of *Phillips' Children's School Questionnaire*

2. Academic Self-Perception—utilized an adjective checklist patterned after the work of Davidson and Lang (1960), although considerable revision was made in this word list

3. Social Distance—utilized a considerably modified version of the scale used by E. Williams (1972), which is a modification of earlier Bogardus-type scales. Social Distance in this present scale is defined in two ways, and thus provides two scores. The first concerns the way members of Racial-Ethnic and Sex subgroups are perceived by the student population as a whole, so that the social distance of a particular class of students is determined. In the other, the individual student indicates his perceived social distance (isolation/closeness) from other students in the school environment. On the former dimension, a higher score indicates greater social distance for members of the class, and each student is assigned the score of his class. In the latter dimension, a higher score indicates perceived closeness rather than isolation. Only this last measure was used in the regression analyses.

4. Locus of Control—utilized the Bialer and Cromwell *Locus of Control Scale*

5. Fourth-Grade Reading achievement—utilized a standardized achievement test administered in fourth grade

6. Intelligence—utilized the CTMM
7. Coping Styles—utilized the variables determining acquiescence, self-enhancement, self-criticalness, and negativism.

The criteria in the regression analyses were reading and mathematics achievement at the end of sixth grade. Regression analyses were carried out using each of these variables in *each* of the eight Racial-Ethnic Status X Sex subgroups.

The efficiency of the models is shown in Table 24, using R^2 as the index of efficiency. Model 1 includes all seven variables, model 2 includes all but Fourth-Grade Reading, model 3 includes all but Fourth-Grade Reading and CTMM, and so on.

Results for the Full Model

We see that model 1 predicts year-end achievement better for females than males, with one exception. Among Mexican-Americans predictability is greater for males. This pattern of sex differences holds for both reading and mathematics.

Mexican-American students are distinguishable in two other ways. The best prediction of reading achievement occurs in this subsample, with 76% of the variance for males and 69% of the variance for females accounted for by the seven variables. This suggests that success in reading among Mexican-American children was especially dependent on psychosituational and personal factors. A corollary finding is that they show the greatest difference between reading and mathematics achievement, with reading achievement being much better predicted. This implies that these predictors are less important in mathematics success, which is in sharp contrast to results in other samples, where reading and mathematics achievement are predicted about equally well.

Table 24 Efficiency of the Models for Predicting Reading and Mathematics Achievement, Using R^2 as Index of Efficiency

Model	Sample					
	Anglo male (N = 180)	Anglo female (N = 167)	Mexican-American male (N = 25)	Mexican-American female (N = 38)	Black male (N = 48)	Black female (N = 73)
Model 1 (all 7 variables)	.51 (.54)	.70 (.64)	.76 (.43)	.69 (.41)	.36 (.31)	.48 (.35)
Model 2 (4th-Grade Reading out)	$.45^+$ $(.41)^+$	$.63^+$ $(.50)^+$	.71 (.38)	.65 (.40)	$.36^*$ $(.20)^*$	$.45^*$ (.34)
Model 3 (4th-Grade CTMM out)	$.14^+$ $(.13)^+$	$.33^+$ $(.26)^†$	$.44^†$ $(.18)^*$	$.57^*$ $(.27)^*$	.31 (.14)	$.08^+$ $(.17)^+$
Model 4 (Locus of Control out)	.13 (.12)	$.23^†$ $(.20)^†$	.42 (.17)	.52 (.22)	$.16^†$ (.13)	.04 $(.12)^*$

Model 5 (Academic Self-Perception out)	.12 (.11)	.22+ (.14)+	.27* (.16)	.43* (.21)	.11 (.05)	.04 (.08)
Model 6 (School Anxiety out)	.05+ (.06)+	.17+ (.09)+	.26 (.10)	.23* (.08)*	.11 (.05)	.02 (.07)
Model 7 (Coping Style out)	.02 (.03)	.03+ (.01)+	.22 (.02)	.06* (.01)	.04 (.03)	.01 (.01)
Model 8 (Social Distance out)	.00* (.00)*	.00* (.00)	.00* (.00)	.00 (.00)	.00 (.00)	.00 (.00)

NOTE: R^2 for mathematics are in parentheses, and symbols *, †, +, refer to F tests comparing a model with the previous model, e.g., model 1 vs. model 2, model 2 vs. model 3, etc.

* p < .05
† p < .01
+ p < .001

**Table 25 Percentage of the Variance in Reading and
Mathematics Achievement Accounted for by Each
Variable**

	Sample					
Variable	Anglo male	Anglo female	Mexican-American male	Mexican-American female	Black male	Black female
4th Grade Reading	6 (13)	7 (14)	5 (5)	4 (1)	0 (11)	3 (1)
4th Grade CTMM	31 (29)	30 (24)	27 (20)	8 (13)	5 (6)	37 (17)
Locus of Control	1 (1)	5 (6)	2 (1)	5 (5)	15 (1)	4 (5)
Academic Self-Perception	1 (1)	6 (6)	15 (1)	9 (1)	5 (8)	0 (4)
School Anxiety	7 (5)	5 (5)	1 (6)	20 (13)	0 (0)	2 (1)
Coping Style	3 (3)	14 (8)	4 (8)	17 (7)	7 (2)	1 (6)
Social Distance	2 (3)	3 (1)	22 (2)	6 (1)	4 (3)	1 (1)

NOTE: Percentages for mathematics are in parentheses.

Model 1 also predicts Black achievement very poorly, with Black males being the lowest of all eight subgroups. Since Black achievement in segregated school settings usually can be predicted about as well as Anglo achievement, the special character of this integrated setting may have contributed to this different outcome. Relevant to this, the overall evidence of the Schilhab study is that Black males had more difficulties adjusting to the Sixth-Grade Learning Center than other students.

These results don't necessarily mean that Black achievement could not be predicted as well, using other variables. But the seven variables utilized include factors previously identified as important in the achievement of minority and other children. It is reasonable, therefore, to raise the possibility that the achievement of Black children may be less predictable in integrated school settings, as they *presently exist.* This may be true because such settings do not accommodate the needs and special problems of Black children as well as they accommodate those of other children.

Contribution of Individual Variables

The role of each variable in reading and mathematics achievement is shown in Table 25. The percentage of the variance accounted for by each of the seven variables is computed for each racial-ethnic subgroup, so that one can determine the relative contribution of each variable to the prediction of achievement in different subgroups.

Summarizing these results, we have the following important findings:

A. *Reading achievement as the criterion*
  1. Anglo males—the CTMM is the best predictor (31%), followed by School Anxiety (7%) and Fourth-Grade Reading (6%)
  2. Anglo females—the CTMM is the best predictor (30%), followed by Coping Style (14%) and Fourth-Grade Reading (7%)
  3. Black males—Locus of Control is the best predictor (15%), followed by Coping Style (7%)

4.   Black females—the CTMM is the best predictor (37%), with no other variable exceeding 4% of the variance

5.   Mexican-American males—the CTMM is the best predictor (27%), followed by Social Distance (22%) and Academic Self-Perception (15%)

6.   Mexican-American females—School Anxiety is the best predictor (20%), followed by Coping Style (17%) and Academic Self-Perception (9%)

B.   *Mathematics achievement as the criterion*

1.   Anglo males—the CTMM is the best predictor (28%), followed by Fourth-Grade Reading (13%) and School Anxiety (5%)

2.   Anglo females—the CTMM is the best predictor (24%), followed by Coping Style (8%) and Fourth-Grade Reading (7%)

3.   Black males—the best predictor is Fourth-Grade Reading (11%), followed by Academic Self-Perception (8%) and the CTMM (6%)

4.   Black females—the CTMM is the best predictor (17%), followed by Coping Style (6%) and Locus of Control (5%)

5.   Mexican-American males—the CTMM is the best predictor (20%), followed by Coping Style (8%) and Fourth-Grade reading (5%)

6.   Mexican-American females—School Anxiety (13%) and CTMM (13%) are the best predictors, followed by Coping Style (7%)

One interesting aspect of these results is the important role of intelligence in these predictions. The CTMM was administered in the fourth grade, 2 years prior to the school year studied, which makes this more fascinating. The effect is not limited to the Anglo subgroups, since the CTMM is the best predictor of reading and mathematics achievement in several of the minority subgroups. The reader should remember, of course, that this outcome may be specific to the context of these particular analyses. If the order of dropping out variables was changed in the regression analyses, this might change the amount of variance in the criterion accounted for by the CTMM. Nevertheless, the results are impressive, and suggest that when integration occurs at a single grade level, and a school includes only such children (in this case, over 500), instructional organization and teaching procedures, etc., may put a premium on intelligence as a factor in academic achievement.

Useful distinction also can be made between the variance accounted for by the two cognitive variables (Fourth-Grade Reading and CTMM), and that accounted for by the remaining, noncognitive variables. With reading achievement as the criterion, cognitive variables account for more than half of the variance accounted for by the full model in all but the two Mexican-American subgroups and the Black males subgroup. Among Black females, only 8% of the total 48% was accounted for by noncognitive variables, in sharp contrast to Black males, where 31% of the total 36% was accounted for by noncognitive variables. The results for mathematics achievement follow this same pattern, except that cognitive variables play more of a role among Black males, less of a role among Black females, and more of a role among Mexican-American males, relative to the role of noncognitive factors.

Specific examination of the noncognitive variables shows that Locus of Control is, significantly, the most important predictor of reading achievement among Black males. This is what we would expect from the literature, although Locus of Control is less important as a predictor of mathematics achievement. Locus of Control also is influential in the mathematics achievement of Black females.

Academic Self-Perception is important in the reading achievement of both Mexican-American subgroups, but it is not as significantly involved in their mathematics achievement. It also enters into the mathematics achievement of Black males.

Coping Style is important in the reading achievement of Anglo females, Black males, and Mexican-American females, while also entering into the mathematics achievement of Anglo females, Black females, and both Mexican-American subgroups. Coping Style is particularly relevant, therefore, to the mathematics achievement of girls.

Social Distance makes only one major contribution, and that is to the reading achievement of Mexican-American males. In this case it makes almost as much of a contribution as the CTMM, which is an intriguing but inexplicable outcome.

School Anxiety is the last of the noncognitive variables, and it is the *best* predictor of reading *and* mathematics achievement among Mexican-American girls. School Anxiety also is the second best predictor for Anglo males, and the third best predictor of their mathematics achievement. It also makes significant contributions in some of the other subgroups, but does not rank as one of the three best predictors in these instances.

In summary, among Anglo children in this integrated single grade school environment, cognitive factors were more important than noncognitive factors, although this was more true of girls than boys. Among minority children there was marked diversity, but noncognitive factors were relatively more important overall, especially for Black males and Mexican-American females.

The significance of these results is enhanced by the fact that, when the effects of a particular predictor were being considered, the related effects of other predictors were statistically controlled. In addition, reading and mathematics achievement can be legitimately considered as crude measures of the *relative amount of academic learning* during the school year. We can conclude therefore that school anxiety had debilitative effects on the academic learning of Anglo children and Mexican-American girls, or at least that the debilitative effects are greater for these subgroups. A corollary to this is that this integrated school environment was less instrumental to the academic learning of Blacks and Mexican-American males, so that the potentially debilitating effects of school anxiety were less apparent in these subgroups. In other words, when the *opportunity* for learning is reduced, so is the opportunity for debilitating factors to exert their full potential impact.

Chapter 5

STRESS, ANXIETY, AND SCHOOL INTERVENTION[1]

Much concern has been expressed in recent years about the proportion of atypical and problem children who are not receiving the psychoeducational services they require to experience school success. While psychologic services are increasingly sought after and available to teachers, too often there is a dichotomy between teachers' conceptions and psychologic services. Teachers see themselves as responsible for the "average" child's cognitive learning, and see responsibility for special affective, personality, or learning problems residing with the school psychologist or some other "expert" to whom the child is referred. Where school psychologists have accepted this traditional role of diagnostician, counselor, or referral resource, there has been little success in infusing psychologic principles into life in classrooms.

A SCHOOL PSYCHOLOGIC-SERVICES MODEL FOR INTERVENTION

A redirection of school psychologic services is needed to deal more effectively with school stress and its undesirable consequences (including anxiety). The impetus for such a reconceptualization is the educational Zeitgeist. The impact of educational technology, the trend toward community-oriented psychologic services (Sarason et al., 1966), the role of psychologic services in educating minorities, the need for evaluation of educational innovations, and the redirection of special education programs all contribute to this Zeitgeist. Moreover, analyses of educational innovations indicate some of the conditions needed for such a reorientation to be successful (Miles, 1964, esp. pp. 631–662).

Reorientation should take into account several propositions. One is that school problems have some relation to the school settings in which they are manifested. This does not necessarily mean that these settings *cause* the problem; it does indicate that the problem is at least "triggered," so that a change in the school setting would change the problem behavior in some way. This emphasizes the need to look closely at the school environment in planning any intervention, and the need to realize that intervention is both descriptive *and* prescriptive. It is important to describe the conditions under which some behavior is acquired, as well as to set forth rules or specify effective ways of achieving change.

The utilization and effectiveness of school psychologic services is increased by *decentralization* and *frequent contacts* with front-line school personnel, especially teachers. That is, such services should be geographically, temporally, and psychologically near to teachers. It is not uncommon for psychologic services personnel to be seen as remote and inaccessible, and for teachers to wait several weeks for action on their referrals. When at least some psychologic services are located in the individual school the time between problem occurrence and action is shortened. Moreover, the psychologic services offered are more apt to include adequate intervention, in addition to diagnosis.

It is important that the aims of psychologic services be *consistent with the goals of schools.* When the psychologist in the schools is oriented toward abnormality and personality development, and the school is oriented toward normality and school learning, the value and impact of school psychologic services is lessened. Moreover, in-service training, etc., should be directed toward the development and utilization of *psychologic resources indigeneous to individual schools.* This includes the training and use of paraprofessionals to provide some psychologic services in the individual school. For example, psychologists can train teachers and parents as behavior modifiers, and use peers as behavior models and tutors.

There also should be an *emphasis on consultation.* Sarason et al. (1966) provide a number of exemplars of this approach in school and other community settings. Recently, the term consultation has become particularly popular with regard to programs dealing with mental health; this has had the effect of reducing the specificity of the term, so that it is misleading to employ the word "consultation" without careful definition. In the present context, consultation is defined as a method in which the psychologist attempts to work with the "care-givers" (Caplan, 1965), and approaches similar to this orientation have been discussed by Iscoe, Pierce-Jones, Friedman, & McGhearty (1967); Gallessich (1974); Newman (1967); and S. B. Sarason et al. (1966). However, we should note that a critical weakness in this area is the lack of related research, although this is changing (Bergan & Tombari, 1975, 1976).

Using as guidelines the mental health profession's conceptualization of the preventive approach, we can identify three types of interventions (Bower, 1965). Primary intervention is that which is applied to the entire population under consideration. Secondary intervention is applied to vulnerable subpopulations, or subpopulations who already manifest some of the early symptoms of dysfunction. Tertiary prevention is applied to subpopulations who have been positively diagnosed as highly dysfunctional (As Cowen [1973] notes, the term "preventive" seems inappropriate, in this instance.)

Hollister (1965) and Phillips, Martin, and Meyers (1972) have used this model to indicate a general conception of a program of interventions in relation to stress in schools. Under primary intervention they suggest: (a) intervening in the environment to eliminate or modify psychologic stress before it has a chance to affect children; and (b) intervening with children to protect them from the impact of psychologic stresses by building up their resistance and personal strengths. As secondary interventions they discuss: (a) interventions for children who are subject to or threatened by stress which can be modified or eliminated; and (b) specific activities for children who need to be isolated from stress that cannot be modified. Finally, for tertiary intervention, they mention specific interventions for children already affected by stress who need immediate mental health "first-aid."

The model identifies several emphases for intervention in relation to school stress. One is to eliminate or modify stress conditions, and this can be done as a preventive, developmental, or remedial measure. Another is to isolate children from stress conditions, which may be applied to vulnerable children or to those who are already stressed. A third one builds up children's resistance to stress, attempting to reduce their vulnerabilities to it. This might involve increasing the child's tolerance for stress, improving his self-esteem, or reducing conflict—to mention just a few possibilities. In the final emphasis, one aims at reducing maladaptive and enhancing adaptive reactions to stress. This can often be done by modifying situational and school task requirements.

In summary, two conceptions of intervention emerge in this analysis. One has its focus on stress itself, and the stress conditions that should be anticipated, identified, and modified for the school system as a whole, for individual schools, within certain subgroups of children, and for individual children. Ultimately, this approach leads to less anxiety, since anxiety is an outgrowth of stress.

The other has its focus on discovering and developing school learning and behavior situations that utilize the advantages and avoid the disadvantages of stress and anxiety. The emphasis in this approach is on mutual relationships between stress, anxiety, and the requirements of school situations and tasks, since these determine whether the effects of stress and anxiety are adaptive or maladaptive.

In an overall sense, these conceptions are complementary since they ultimately lead to systematic efforts to develop school learning environments that minimize stress and reduce its undesirable effects. Of course, such efforts can proceed successfully only if they are accompanied by concerted research programs and educational change strategies, which up to now have been lacking.

School Culture, Educational Change Processes, and School Intervention Programs

As S. B. Sarason (1972) points out, "changing the school setting in any way for the purpose of controlling, or diluting, or eliminating the debilitating effects of anxiety requires far more than a theory of anxiety." In other words, understanding the nature of school stress, and relating its maladaptive consequences to a school psychologic services model and specific intervention strategies is not enough.

One must integrate such understanding with an in-depth comprehension of the school as a social organization or system. To put the matter succinctly, one needs a theory of school culture in conjunction with a theory of the change process in order to plan and implement school interventions.

Characteristics of Life in School Settings as a Part of School Culture

The "hidden curriculum" is an important part of school life, and as Jackson (1968) and others have noted, too much attention is paid to the academic demands of schooling, which might be called the "official" curriculum, rather than to institutional expectations. Neverthless, the student, teacher, *and* school psychologist must master both curriculums if they are to succeed.

Life in classrooms is highly standardized, and there is considerable uniformity and regularity in the physical environment. This also is true of academic activities and the social atmosphere of the classroom. However, there is variety amid the constancy, as when specific content and subject matter changes from day to day in a schedule that assigns certain periods to particular activities throughout the school year.

Life in classrooms also involves a great deal of crowding. Most of the things done in classrooms are done with others, or at least in the presence of others. The classroom is an intimate place as well, since children are in such close proximity for long periods of time. There is probably no place else in society where groups are regularly brought together for long periods of time under such intimate conditions.

In addition, classrooms are basically evaluative settings where not only what you do but what others think you do is important. In effect, evaluation is a constant condition of life in classrooms that the student has to learn to live with. While evaluation is encountered in other environments in society, nowhere does it have the ubiquitousness it has in the school environment.

Lastly, the school is a place where there is a sharp division of power. Authority resides in the teacher and students are relatively powerless to shape classroom events. This unequalness of power is frequently overlooked in discussions of the nature of schooling, but it is a fact that has indisputable consequences.

Extrapolating from such features of life in classrooms leads one to identify elements of school culture. That is to say, as one examines the total pattern of school life and its products embodied in thought, speech, actions, beliefs, and social norms, one is discovering school culture.

Characteristics of Teachers

Another important element in school culture is the classroom teacher. There obviously is a relationship between the teachers' work and the institutional framework in which they and their students are embedded. It also is evident that teachers contribute to and are a part of school culture, as well as being influenced by it.

Systematic observation and personal contacts with teachers has revealed a lot about how the teachers see and evaluate themselves, how they view life in the classroom and institutional authority, and what satisfactions they derive from their work as teachers. It also appears that certain themes are more general than these specific types of information, and illuminate important aspects of school culture.

One of the characteristics of teachers is their orientation to the here-and-now, or the present. In the teachers' view, the results of teaching are quite immediate, and they are prone to use fleeting behavioral cues to ascertain how well they are doing in their job. For example, the visible signs of alertness and enthusiasm among their students tell them how well a particular lesson has gone over.

In contrast, the students' performance on tests is given little emphasis, and teachers give testing only minor importance in determining how well they have done. This seems to indicate a pervasive mistrust of tests, especially among elementary teachers. As a consequence, few teachers see objective achievement tests as intrinsically related to teaching effectiveness or professional satisfaction.

Their views of relations to students and school authority are also important teacher characteristics. Many teachers try to be informal in the classroom, and identify relations that are formal as "old-fashioned." In addition, they are concerned about professional autonomy, and see their relations to superiors as more formal than desired. Moreover, they express concern over the prospect of being observed too frequently, and about the threat of too many curricular controls. They see both these actions as inimical to professionalism.

The satisfactions of teaching are closely tied to individual students, rather than to the success of the class as a whole. There is a sense of urgency, as well as a missionary spirit, in the work of the teacher, especially at the elementary level. As a consequence, unexpected transformations of individual students result in the greatest feelings of personal accomplishment.

In interpreting these broad themes, Jackson (1968) makes the additional observations that teachers are characterized by an overly simplified view of causality, by an intuitive rather than a rational approach to classroom events, and by an accepting attitude toward the educational status quo. Thus, teachers are not only a part of the institutionalized life of the school; they also stand for qualities that extend beyond the boundaries of school culture. In essence, while contributing to school culture in many ways, they at the same time transcend it. This is why they have the potential for changing the school culture, *if they so desire.* It is the realization of this, and its implications for intervention, that make the foregoing characteristics of the teacher so important.

Toward a Theory of Educational Change

The truth about educational innovations is that most eventually are unsuccessful in achieving their intended results (Miles, 1964). In spite of this, some generalizations have been produced about educational innovations, although no systematically drawn theory of educational change is possible.

The nature of the educational system itself influences innovation rates. Generally, innovation diffusion rates within education are slower than those in industrial and other systems. One reason for this is the lack of change agents to promote new educational ideas. Another is the lack of economic incentives to adopt innovations.

It also appears that certain ideological beliefs in the teaching profession serve to block innovations. For example, beliefs that the teacher is an autonomous professional, when in actuality he or she is a functionary in a bureaucracy, has a restrictive effect on innovation.

Turning to the innovation itself, educational innovations are almost never installed on their merits (Miles, 1964). Yet it seems likely that some characteristics of the innovation—e.g., its cost, availability of supportive materials, difficulty of its use, and its degree of congruence with the system—are factors in its installation within an educational system. In addition, an innovation that is perceived as relatively nonthreatening and easy to institutionalize is more likely to be accepted.

Most innovations appear also to be stimulated, shepherded, and nurtured by some active person or group either internal or external to the system. In many instances, however, the initiation of change comes from outside the system, although the innovator must establish viable contacts within the system.

Finally, there are certain prior conditions within the educational system and the larger community that facilitate change. In every system there are stability-maintaining forces as well as internal pressures for change. For example, other factors being equal, an educational system that has a relatively large number of tenured professionals, and has hierarchically arranged subsystems within the overall organization, is less susceptible to change. Factors in the community and the society at large, however, appear to be accelerating educational change. As special examples of such pressures one may cite competition with the Soviet Union, especially after Sputnik, and pressures from the Black people of the country. In this connection, S. B. Sarason's (1971) analyses should be consulted, since such educational changes may be more apparent than real. In general, periods of rapid social change are also periods of accelerated educational change.

Planning and Implementing Educational Change

Installing an innovation in an educational system is a developmental rather than a mechanical process, for during the installation both the innovation and the system are altered (Miles, 1964) Generally, most attention is put on the innovation itself, and the planning, experimental work, and other details of implementing the innovation are slighted.

A change strategy, in contrast to specific tactics, usually relies on a number of principles for success. One of these is the use of "multiplier effects," as, for example, when extra communication channels are opened up in the system. Other examples are organizing special groups to aid in diffusion efforts, and teaching system members how to use the innovation.

Another change strategy is to introduce change-inducing changes, i.e., changes that will lead to further changes. For example, a citizen's survey might be organized, outside consultants might be used, and/or new organizational structures might be developed.

Finally, there appear to be optimal conditions within the stages of the change processes for effective innovation. First, credibility is an important factor, since there frequently are discrepancies between public communications about an intended innovation and private reactions to it. With regard to this problem, peer communication networks are especially helpful, e.g., teachers are most apt to trust what other teachers have to say who have tried the innovation or have had some prior involvement with it.

With respect to evaluation, the potential user often assesses a proposed innovation in terms of its apparent net consequences to him and others he is concerned about. Thus a highly impersonal and scientific approach to educational change, where there is only objective assessment of the pros and cons of an innovation, is apt to be ineffective.

Innovating groups themselves must form close linkages with the target system, as previously noted. At the same time, within such groups there should be high involvement, commitment, mutual identification, free communication, norms supporting change, and full use of member resources. In summary, the innovating group needs to be an effectively functioning group.

Summary

Studies of educational change, as summarized by Miles (1964) and others, and studies of the school culture by S. B. Sarason (1971, 1972) and others, provide a number of insights and generalizations. But unfortunately, there is still no theory of educational change or of school culture in systematically developed form. Nevertheless, we do know something about these phenomena. Therefore, in school interventions relating to stress and anxiety reactions, one should be aware of this, and make what use one can of what is known. To do otherwise would be indefensible.

INTERVENTION STRATEGIES

"Resocialization"

Stressed and anxious children need to be "resocialized," especially in the primary grades, into modes of acting, thinking, and feeling that are more compatible with school expectations. To offset the effects of stress and anxiety there is a need to work with such children to establish basic strategies for dealing with information, habits of attention, and reflective styles of behavior.

One important aspect of such "resocialization" is the realization that stress reactions are individual differences that can be useful in designing educational "treatments," even though few aptitude–treatment interaction effects have been demonstrated (Bracht, 1970). For this to be effective, therefore, close attention will have to be given to the stress coping *processes,* since it is not enough to identify a set of variables that help predict performance. One must also tell how the child should be trained, or how the stressful situation should be changed, to improve his performance.

Another critical aspect of the design of "treatments" for maladaptive stress reactions is finding a way of matching cognitive demands to the child's current level of competence. Task difficulty interacts with anxiety level so as to be particularly detrimental when tasks are too difficult. Optimum matching of instruction to development is difficult, however, due to lack of detailed knowledge of the interrelation of stress, anxiety, and difficulty (and other task characteristics). In this situation, teachers should permit anxious children some degree of choice of tasks, rather than make them rely on rigorous prescription by the teacher.

The distinction between the design of the school learning environment and the development of specific teaching components is also useful. Optimizing learning by focusing on strategies of lesson design or teaching specific learning objectives is not apt to be as helpful to the stressed and anxious child as the systematic programming of the classroom environment. In essence, the teacher working with stressed, anxious children should emphasize general cognitive, affective, and behavioral "resocialization," giving attention to the school environmental conditions that facilitate socioemotional as well as mental development.

Crisis Prevention Techniques

According to Bower (1964) and others, there are crisis situations common to subpopulations in the schools. One example is first-graders beginning their formal school experience, and another is adolescents entering junior high school. A crisis is simply a struggle with a stressful situation, and how one copes with crises is the important thing. For example, Caplan (1965) considers the response to these rather infrequent situations of central importance in the development of personality.

Although we have a gross idea of crisis situations in school from Bower (1964) and others, specific research is needed to identify in greater detail what aspects of such situations produce stress and anxiety. In addition, we need to learn about other situations during the school year that typically introduce important crises.

Bower (1964) has proposed a specific program, utilizing this approach with regard to the school entrance crisis. According to Bower, at school entrance the child anxiously searches for the rules that govern this new activity. Therefore, some supportive coaching can be helpful at this time.

One aspect of this program is an assessment of each child prior to school entry, so that effective planning can be done. This assessment would include an evaluation of cognitive, social, and emotional characteristics. Both parents would ideally attend weekly meetings with other parents in order to keep in touch with their children's progress. A school social worker, counselor, or psychologist would be assigned to families requiring help at this point, and would work with them through a planning period. In this way it is hoped that the child and family will from the beginning experience school as an institution that is ready to meet the needs of its students, and more importantly, they will have an opportunity to meet a stressful transition in a strengthening and integrating manner.

Psychologic Inoculation

Another way to deal with stressful situations would be what might be called psychologic "inoculation." This technique is consistent with interruption theory (Mandler & Watson, 1966), in that an unpleasant experience becomes less stressful as it is incorporated as part of one's cognitive plan.

The basic approach is twofold. First, if we can provide knowledge regarding a stressful situation, then we will prevent a part of the threat that results from uncertainty. Second, if we can provide help in the development of techniques for coping, then we eliminate the need for passive endurance and encourage active and constructive participation in the situation. This channeling of stress into constructive avenues should also help to reduce anxiety.

One example might be to provide information prior to examinations that clearly delineates what the test will be like, and also furnishes guidelines to help students develop precise methods of preparation. If we could prevent some of the stress of test taking and help channel energies into specific and useful methods of study, it might help develop tests that are the effective learning instruments they can be.

Incorporate Psychologic Principles into the Curriculum

A considerable amount of work has been done to encourage the teaching of psychologic principles in the schools. Although some have proposed the development of a specific course in psychology (Roen, 1967), it is even more significant to introduce psychologic concepts into the overall school curriculum (Ojemann, 1961; Zimiles, 1967; Phillips & DeVault, 1959; Farr, 1967). However, there are few widely accepted and implementable programs in the socioemotional area. Four that are available and have special relevance to school stress and anxiety are:

1.   The "causal" approach (Ojemann, 1961, 1969) is aimed at helping children become more sensitive to the reasons behind behavior, and identify and consider alternative solutions to problems. In addition, there is research evidence that the causal approach produces desirable changes in children in relation to stress reactions (Muuss, 1960; Ojemann & Snider, 1964).

2.   The Human Development Program (Bessell & Palomares, 1969) is based on the assumption that children who achieve mastery and gain approval in social relations will develop healthy personalities. Dispelling the "delusion of uniqueness" also is a part of the program, as is emphasizing "inclusion, control, and affection" in interpersonal relations. Its creators see it as a preventive mental health program, and the main procedure for implementing the program is the daily "Magic Circle" meetings. Unfortunately, no studies of the effects of the program on stress reactions could be located.

3.   Reality Therapy (Glasser, 1969), whose adherents

insist that schools must eliminate failure, seeks to bring about this change by training every teacher to use Reality Therapy techniques. The mechanism for using these techniques is the class meeting, and social problem-solving and open-ended, educational types of meetings are utilized as springboards for the use of Reality Therapy. To the writer's knowledge, no carefully designed evaluations of the program have been reported, although there are a number of circulated testimonials from satisfied users.

4. Dinkmeyer's (1971) "Developing Understanding of Self and Others" program is a sequential series of activities for developing the child's understanding of self and others. Materials for the program are attractively packaged and self-contained, but the few experimental studies of the program's effects (Eldridge, Barcikowski, & Witmer, 1973; Koval & Hales, 1972) have produced equivocal results

Overall, such programs are promising innovations and preventive approaches to school stress and anxiety. It also is obvious that such programs (with the exception of Ojemann's) have not been sufficiently researched. In addition, with regard to the purposes of this chapter, all the programs lack detailed descriptions of how to implement the ideas presented.

Establishing Supportive Resources to Regular Classes

One current technique that attempts to deal with severely maladaptive stress reactions in children is placement in special education classes. But as psychologists and educators, we must be cognizant of the subtle effects of this sort of labeling. The child who finds that he was unsuccessful in a regular class, and then finds himself in a group containing other children who are marked as failures in school, is not likely to maintain or develop aspirations or expectations commensurate with his ability. In addition, the attitude of special education teachers is frequently pessimistic, for they do not expect to be able to help change children who have already been labeled "uncontrollable," "emotionally disturbed," or "mentally retarded."

A factor that tends to increase these problems in utilizing special education classes and techniques is that the orientation is sometimes custodial. In other words, this type of educational placement is sometimes seen as providing a place to keep the "problem child" until he is no longer required to attend school. It is not surprising, therefore, that students in special education classes have been found to be burdened with feelings of rejection, hostility, and anger toward the school, which are probably over and above the feelings associated with the school difficulties they have previously experienced (Hunter, 1968).

Moreover, there is frequently a neglect of planning to return the child to the regular classroom in cases where this is ultimately feasible. Again, it would appear that by neglecting this possibility we are communicating in a subtle manner to the child that he is not expected to move out of the special class. Thus one significant improvement in special education classes might be to incorporate in the general philosophy of special education, as well as in the specific procedures of placement, etc., some plans for return to the regular class, and for follow-up activities with the child and his regular classroom teacher after returning (Lewis, 1967; Morse, Cutler, & Fink, 1964; Tolor & Lane, 1968).

We have pointed out several weaknesses of special education classes; yet we still recognize that there are some children in school who are so burdened by problems that it is necessary to do something, and the regular classroom does not seem to have the resources to handle these children without outside support. One potential approach to these problems is the Diagnostic–Intervention class (Ebert, Dain, & Phillips, 1970; Phillips, 1967a, 1968). As this program has been described by Phillips, it would have a psychoeducational orientation. This is particularly important in light of the work of Morse et al. (1964), which finds that the psychoeducational orientation to special education is most effective. In recent years the "least restrictive alternative" concept has gained increased acceptance through court and legislative actions, so that many state and local plans have been modified to educate more children in regular classrooms, with resource rooms and other supportive services used as backup.

Behavior Modification

The application of systematic reinforcement contingencies in school is especially appropriate in the case of the stressed and anxious child. The use of praise or other forms of attention from the teacher or peers, token economies, and contingency "contracts" all have been frequently and successfully used, and a few studies have appeared that examine the effects of self-administered reinforcement, which may be even more effective (Johnson, 1970; Lovitt & Curtis, 1969).

Such efforts should not focus only on decreasing disruptive behavior and increasing attention to tasks, but also should emphasize learning and academic performance. In addition, a great deal of attention should be given to how the reinforcement program is terminated and the behavior maintained by contingencies existing in the "normal" school environment (Resnick, 1971).

Obviously, generalization of desirable behavior changes, from the remediating environment (e.g., a diagnostic–intervention classroom) to other settings in which the child operates, is a difficult problem. Two studies suggest that practical and effective use can be made of peers in producing generalized behaviors (Johnston & Johnston, 1972; Walker & Buckley, 1972).

Specific Aptitude Training

Aptitude training may be a means of adapting to the anxious child's weaknesses, and therefore enhancing his ability to profit from instruction. What is suggested, in other words, is a strategy that treats aptitudes as dependent variables, and seeks to influence them through instructional intervention. In this way it is possible, by specifically exercising aptitudes weakened by the influence of stress reactions (including anxiety), to enhance the child's learning ability.

One way to approach this is through social modeling and the influence of the teacher. Another is to use the controlling function of self-speech or self-guidance procedures, so that stressed, anxious children are taught to covertly talk to themselves and in this way modify their problem-solving, task behavior (Meichenbaum & Goodman, 1969). Such self-talk can also be related to mathemagenic activities with respect to the learning of written materials, including activities such as set, habits of attention, rehearsal, etc. (Rothkopf, 1970).

Task Instructions, Sequencing, Difficulty, and Other Characteristics

Recent studies indicate that predictions about the effect of anxiety on school performance are difficult. High anxiety is not necessarily detrimental to learning, and its effects depend on a number of factors, including defense mechanisms, task difficulty, sex differences, and the sequencing of tasks. Nevertheless, in attempts to reduce the possibly debilitating effects of anxiety, two approaches have been used. One approach attempts to reduce the anxiety, and the other attempts to help the anxious learner by providing supportive aids for the detrimental processes produced by anxiety.

With respect to anxiety reduction, possibly helpful strategies include the use of "reassurance" in task instructions, etc. (I. G. Sarason, 1958); and role playing (Chesler & Fox, 1966). Examples of the second approach might include: the use of "task orientation" and "motivating task instructions" (I. G. Sarason, 1972); providing memory support (Sieber, 1969); and reducing task difficulty (O'Neil, Spielberger, & Hansen, 1969).

Although the empiric results are complex or equivocal, programmed instruction also offers advantages in dealing with stress and anxiety in school. Tobias and Williamson (1968) hypothesize that programmed instruction minimizes personal evaluation, reduces difficulty, and decreases the stress caused by uncertainty. S. B. Sarason et al., (1960) also discuss the importance of stressful aspects of personal evaluation, especially with regard to the anxious student.

In a programmed-learning approach, tasks are well structured and clearly defined, so that we would expect less stress as a result of ambiguity. In addition, the use of structure and moderately graded learning steps might be brought to bear on the learning environment in a number of ways.

Therapeutic Tutoring

Therapeutic tutoring is a psychoanalytically-oriented remedial approach to children with "primary neurotic learning inhibitions" (Prentice & Sperry, 1965). This approach focuses neither on the learning disability itself, nor on the presumed underlying conflicts. Instead, both the educational and therapeutic functions are retained, and are strategically interrelated.

The role of the therapeutic tutor requires a knowledge of the usual remediation methods, as well as a knowledge of psychodynamics. In addition, the therapeutic tutor should be ingenious and innovative, so that his or her tutorial efforts combine educational and psychodynamic principle in an effective way.

Some teaching experience combined with the skills of a school or child/clinical psychologist would usually be necessary to fill this role. However, other professionals, even paraprofessionals, may be suitable, especially if a school or child/clinical psychologist is available for supervision and consultation.

Modeling and Incidental Learning

The effects of modeling on behavior have not been widely reported in relation to stress and anxiety. Special attention should be paid to studies by Geer and Turtelbaub (1967) and DeWolfe (1967), which found that the observation of a model reduced anxiety. Specifically, DeWolfe reported that identifying with a model who showed little fear in a stress-producing situation was associated with decreased fear in the subject. Though less relevant, I. G. Sarason, Pederson, and Nyman (1968) found that observing a model succeeding on a serial learning task significantly increased the subject's task performance, and Ross (1966) found that high-dependent children showed more evidence of incidental learning through imitation.

One problem that occurs with modeling behavior and with general incidental learning is that anxiety has been found to reduce the subject's use of incidental cues (Easterbrook, 1959). This would imply that high-anxiety students would need aids to ensure that they focus on important incidental cues. Other work by Frase (1967), Pyper (1969), and Rothkopf (1966) suggests ways to circumvent the reduced cue utilization associated with anxiety.

An interesting extension of the concept of modeling is learning from verbal instructions, i.e., from being told what to do. Bandura (1971) calls instructions verbal models, and points out how they have an instigational function (i.e., getting performance started) and a modeling function (describing the action required). Since it appears that stress and anxiety have a greater negative impact at the initial stage of tasks, such efforts may be especially useful. For example, there is a negative relation between anxiety and the quality of immediate recall, perhaps because anxiety creates distracting stimulation that deflects attention from relevant information.

Psychotherapy and Counseling

One way to reduce the negative effects of stress and anxiety would be to permit children to express dependent needs (S. B. Sarason et al., 1960). For example, in an individual testing situation an anxious student does better because of the personal relationship and the opportunity to express dependency. This would not be the case in a group test. Similar analogies can be drawn to other test and testlike classroom situations, although it would appear that the limits of this concept's generalizability require further research.

Recently there has been much discussion regarding the use of sensitivity training. Harrison (1966) indicates that sensitivity training increases the level of personal functioning of anxious persons (Goldstein & Dean, 1966). Similarly, there have been studies that discussed the efficacy of group therapy with children (Feder, 1967) and group therapy with parents (Gildea et al., 1967), while Axline (1949), Bills (1950), and Mehus (1953) have demonstrated that play therapy helped to reduce children's problems in reading. Furthermore, Wolpe (1966) has written extensively on the advantages of behavior therapy and his techniques of reciprocal inhibition, counterconditioning, desensitization, etc.

An Integrated, Programmatic Approach to School Stress and Anxiety

Although a number of intervention strategies have been suggested, an integrated approach, utilizing various strategies in combination, is likely to have special value. Such a program is outlined below. Its focus is on self-preoccupation and avoidance behavior, two major debilitative characteristics of anxious children, and on the development of coping with stress skills.

Dealing with Self-Preoccupation

As I. G. Sarason (1975a) notes, much anxiety involves self-preoccupation characterized by heightened self-awareness, self-doubt, and self-depreciation. These cognitive activities exert a negative impact on both overt behavior and physiologic activity. In addition, self-preoccupation interferes with information processing at three levels: (1) attention to environmental cues; (2) encoding and transformation of these data; and (3) selection of overt response. Therefore, self-preoccupied children need to gain better control over their self-oriented thinking and thus to become more adept at coping in stressful situations.

Intervention can deal directly with these problems, and a promising approach is cognitive training. Applied to test-taking stress, for example, the components of such training might include:

1. Information—applicable information about studying and test-taking skills
2. Modeling—opportunity to observe someone take tests, or to think through testlike problems
3. Self-monitoring and self-control—especially of behavior and thought in test-taking situations

4. Attentional training—practice in attending to the task at hand

5. Relaxation—learning how to relax under specified conditions

6. Practice and reinforcement—this needs to be done to shape adaptive functioning.

Reducing Avoidance Behavior

Avoidance behavior, which is quite common among stressed and anxious children, can be most effectively reduced by a coping, self-verbalizing model (Meichenbaum, 1971). The model's coping consists of initially demonstrating fearful behavior, then modeling coping behavior, and finally showing mastery behavior. The use of coping behavior is based on the assumption that increased similarity between the observer (i.e., the child) and the model facilitates imitating, as well as detailed modeling of how to cope. The addition of the model's self-verbalizations will usually result in greater behavioral change.

Specific procedures to follow in developing a program utilizing filmed sequences to deal with avoidance behavior in children include:

1. Showing multiple models' performances under a variety of graded threatening experiences, with the model performing a graduated sequence of activities, using several feared objects that vary in given characteristics, so as to increase generalization

2. Systematic verbalization by models of coping strategies, e.g., effective use of relaxation through slow breathing to overcome fear

3. Allowing the subject (i.e., the child who is observing) to have control of the rate of presentation of modeling stimuli by regulating the graduated film sequence, assuming the models are presented via film.

Developing Skills for Coping with Stress

In later research Meichenbaum, Turk, and Burstein (1975) have dealt with the nature of coping with stress. They describe the sequence of steps that characterizes the process of coping with stressors as:

1. Preparatory steps toward coping—cognitive preparation in the form of "work of worrying," which includes the anticipatiory fear and mental rehearsal essential for developing self-delivered reassurances. The work of worrying is conceptualized as inner preparation increasing the level of tolerance for subsequent threat.

2. Coping acts themselves—the physical acts the child can engage in to prepare for stressors, as well as the physical manipulation of the environment allowing physical defense, escape, etc. Cognitive manipulations that can also be utilized to create an impression of safety, security, or gratification are what the child attends to, how he integrates both external and internal environment, and how he assesses his own capabilities of coping.

With this orientation to coping skills, several guidelines for training children in coping with stress and anxiety are available. First of all, coping techniques must be flexible to meet diverse situations. Training techniques also must be sensitive to individual, cultural, and situational differences. In addition, coping strategies are successful when they reduce anxiety, and therefore lead to more adaptive coping responses. Finally, exposure during training to less threatening stress- and anxiety-producing events is beneficial.

The training program itself may be viewed as having two phases, which should be characterized by certain activities. The educational phase of training must provide a conceptual framework for understanding the nature of stressful reactions. This must be plausible to the child, and provide the child with the logic of the training that follows. The rehearsal phase of training provides a variety of direct action and cognitive coping techniques. This can include assessing the reality of the situation and controlling negative thoughts through the use of self-statements The child also needs to acknowledge the arousal experienced, and "psych" himself up to cope with the stressful situation. In addition, the child should reinforce himself for successful coping and employ the coping skills learned under other stressful conditions.

A Cognitive and Multimodal Approach

Richardson's (1976) anxiety management program also has considerable relevance in working with anxious elementary-school-age children. His proposed program would rely more heavily on role playing and behavior rehearsal rather than on extended discussion and rational analysis. The major components of such a program would be:

1. Promoting *awareness of the nature of anxiety and stress and different ways of coping with them*—would utilize prescriptive role playing and ensuing discussion to promote awareness.

2. *Relaxation training*—would be taught as a self-management skill. Practice in differential relaxation, as well as encouragement and assignments to practice at home and school would be included.

3. Development of *plans and skills for more effective coping*—would involve writing down adaptive self-talk and beliefs; time, individual attention, role playing, and simple products would be emphasized.

4. Intensive *practice in stress and anxiety management*—would include anxiety induction and relaxation, role playing of standardized and individualized coping with stress,

and imaginal practice of standardized and individualized coping behavior.

CONCLUDING COMMENT

Succinct summary remarks for an area as complex as this one present a difficult task. The school intervention area in general lacks clear articulation and empiric footing, and this chapter itself rests too heavily on soft, insufficient data and impressions of the author and others who are cited. The fact of the matter, though, is that schools must do something about children's stress and anxiety and their maladaptive consequences. And even if some of the interventions proposed turn out to be only palliative, they do focus attention on specific aspects of the problem, and the possibilities for preventive, developmental, and remedial action. Even if such frameworks and strategies do not effectively handle stress and anxiety problems, it is hoped that there will be a reexaminiation of assumptions and a consideration and implementation of alternatives. And ultimately, the research base that is developed in this process will be crucial to the designing of more effective interventions for the pressing and unresolved problem of stress and anxiety in school.

NOTES

Some portions of this chapter are based on an earlier analysis of interventions in relation to anxiety in school by Phillips, Martin, and Meyers (1972).

REFERENCES

Adams, E., & Sarason, I. G. Relation between anxiety in children and their parents. *Child Development,* 1963, **34,** 237–246.

Adams, R. A., & Phillips, B. N. Factors associated with under- and overachievement among socio-economically and racial-ethnically different elementary school children. *Psychology in the Schools,* 1968, **5,** 170–174.

Adams, R. A., & Phillips, B. N. *Anxiety, birth order, and sociometric choices among elementary school children.* Paper presented at the annual meeting of the Southwestern Psychological Association, Arlington, Texas, April 1966.

Atkinson, J. W., & Feather, N. T. Review and appraisal. In J. W. Atkinson & N. T. Feather (Eds.), *A theory of achievement motivation.* New York: Wiley, 1966.

Axline, V. Play therapy: A way of understanding and helping reading problems. *Childhood Education,* 1949, **26,** 156–161.

Bandura, A. Vicarious and self-reinforcement processes. In R. Glasser (Ed.), *The nature of reinforcement.* New York: Academic Press, 1971.

Bereiter, C. Some persistent dilemmas in the measurement of change. In C. H. Harris (Ed.), *Problems in measuring change.* Madison: University of Wisconsin Press, 1963.

Bergan, J. R., & Tombari, M. L. Consultant skill and efficiency and the implementation and outcomes of consultation. *Journal of School Psychology,* 1976, **14,** 3–14.

Bergan, J. R., & Tombari, M. L. The analysis of verbal interactions occurring during consultation. *Journal of School Psychology*, 1975, **13**, 209–226.

Bessell, H., & Palomares, U. H. *Human development program.* Los Angeles: Vulcan Binders, 1969.

Bills, R. Nondirective play therapy with retarded readers. *Journal of Consulting Psychology*, 1950, **14**, 140–149.

Blanchard, P. Psychoanalytic contributions to the problem of reading difficulty. In A. Freud, H. Hartman & E. Kris (Eds.), *Psychoanalytic study of the child.* New York: International Universities Press, Inc., 1946.

Bovard, E. W. The effects of social stimuli on the response to stress. *Psychological Bulletin*, 1959, **66**, 267–277.

Bower, E. M. The modification, mediation, and utilization of stress during the school years. *American Journal of Orthopsychiatry*, 1964, **34**, 667–674.

Bower, E. M. Primary prevention of mental and emotional disorders: A frame of reference. In N. Lambert (Ed.), *The protection and promotion of mental health in schools.* (Mental Health Monograph No. 5) Washington, D.C.: United States Government Printing Office, 1965.

Bracht, G. H. Experimental factors related to aptitude-treatment interaction. *Review of Educational Research*, 1970, **40**, 627–645.

Caplan, G. Opportunities for school psychologists in the primary prevention of mental disorders in children. In N. Lambert (Ed.), *The protection and promotion of mental health in schools.* (Mental Health Monograph No. 5.) Washington, D.C.: United States Government Printing Office, 1965.

Caplan, G. *The theory and practice of mental health consultation.* New York: Basic Books, 1970.

Castenada, S., McCandless, B. R., & Palermo, D. S. The children's form of the manifest anxiety scale. *Child Development*, 1956, **27**, 317–326.

Cattell, R. B. Anxiety and motivation: Theory and crucial experiments. In C. D. Spielberger (Ed.), *Anxiety and behavior.* New York: Academic Press, 1966.

Cattell, R., & Scheier, I. The nature of anxiety: A review of thirteen multivariate analyses comprising 814 variables. *Psychological Review*, 1958, **4**, 351–388.

Cattell, R., & Scheier, I. *The meaning and measurement of neuroticism and anxiety.* New York: Ronald Press, 1961.

Chandler, G. E. *An investigation of school anxiety and nongraded classroom organization.* Unpublished doctoral dissertation, University of Texas, Austin, 1969.

Chesler, M., & Fox, R. *Role playing methods in the classroom.* Chicago: Science Research Associates, 1966.

Cohen, A. M., & Forest, J. R. Organizational behavior and adaptations to organizational change of sensitizer and represser problem-solving groups. *Journal of Personality and Social Psychology,* 1968, **8,** 209–216.

Coleman, J. S., Campbell, E. Q., Hobson, C. J., McPartland, J., Mood, A. M., Weinfeld, F. D., & York, R. L. *Equality of educational opportunity.* (U.S.O.E.) Washington, D.C.: United States Government Printing Office, 1966.

Cowen, E. L. Social and community interventions. In P. Mussen & R. Rosenzweig (Eds.), *Annual review of psychology.* Palo Alto, Calif.: Annual Reviews, Inc., 1973.

Davidson, H. H., & Lang, G. Children's perceptions of their teachers' feelings toward them related to self-perception, school achievement and behavior. *Journal of Experimental Education,* 1960, **27,** 107–118.

Davidson, K. S. Interviews of parents of high-anxious and low-anxious children. *Child Development,* 1959, **30,** 341–351.

Denny, J. P. Effects of anxiety and intelligence on concept formation. *Journal of Experimental Psychology,* 1966, **72,** 596–602.

DeWolfe, A. S. Identification and fear decrease. *Journal of Consulting Psychology,* 1967, **31,** 259–263.

Dinkmeyer, D. Top priority: Understanding self and others. *The Elementary School Journal,* 1971, **72,** 62–71.

Dreikurs, R. *Psychology in the classroom.* (2nd ed.) New York: Harper & Row, 1968.

Dunn, J. A. Factor structure of the test anxiety scale for children. *Journal of Consulting Psychology,* 1964, **28,** 92.

Dunn, J. A. Stability of the factor structure of the test anxiety scale for children across age and sex groups. *Journal of Consulting Psychology,* 1965, **29,** 187.

Dunn, J. A. The approach-avoidance model for the analysis of school anxiety. *Journal of Educational Psychology,* 1968, **59,** 388–394.

Easterbrook, J. A. The effect of emotion on cue utilization and the organization of behavior. *Psychological Review,* 1959, **66,** 183–201.

Ebert, D. W., Dain, R. N., & Phillips, B. N. An attempt at implementing the diagnosis-intervention class model. *Journal of School Psychology,* 1970, **8,** 191–196.

Eldridge, M. S., Barcikowski, R. S., & Witmer, J. M. Effects of DUSO on the self-concepts of second grade students. *Elementary School Guidance and Counseling,* 1973, **7,** 256–260.

Endler, N. S., & O'Sada, M. A multi-dimensional measure of trait anxiety: The S-R inventory of general trait anxiousness. *Journal of Consulting and Clinical Psychology*, 1975, **43**, 319–329.

Erikson, E. H. *Childhood and society.* New York: Norton, 1950.

Farr, A. L. *A cognitive approach to promoting more effective personal functioning in third grade children.* Unpublished doctoral dissertation. University of Texas, Austin, 1967.

Feder, C. Z. Relationship of repression-sensitization to adjustment status, social desirability, and acquiescence response set. *Journal of Consulting Psychology*, 1967, **31**, 401–406.

Feld, S., & Lewis, J. Further evidence on the stability of the factor structure of the test anxiety scale for children. *Journal of Consulting Psychology*, 1967, **31**, 434.

Finch, A. J., Jr., Kendall, P. C., Montgomery, L. E. & Morris, T. Effects of two types of failure on anxiety. *Journal of Abnormal Psychology*, 1975, **84**, 583–585.

Fiske, D. W., & Pearson, P. H. Theory and techniques of personality measurement. In P. Mussen & R. Rosenzweig (Eds.), *Annual review of psychology.* Palo Alto, Calif.: Annual Reviews, Inc., 1970.

Forbes, D. W. *An experimental study of the effect of threat and anxiety on concept formation.* Paper presented at the annual meeting of the American Educational Research Association, Los Angeles, February 1969.

Frase, L. T., Learning from prose material: Length of passage, knowledge of results, and position of questions. *Journal of Educational Psychology*, 1967, **58**, 266–272.

Freud, A. *The problem of anxiety.* New York: Psychoanalytic Quarterly Press & Norton, 1936.

Freud, A. *An outline of psychoanalysis.* New York: Norton, 1949.

Gallessich, J. Training the school psychologist for consultation. *Journal of School Psychology*, 1974, **12**, 138–149.

Geer, J. H., & Turtelbaub, A. Fear reduction following observation of a model. *Journal of Personality and Social Psychology*, 1967, **6**, 327–332.

Gildea, M. C., Glidewell, J. C., & Kantor, M. B. The St. Louis school mental health project: History and evaluation. In E. Cowen, E. Gardner, & M. Zax (Eds.), *Emergent approaches to mental health problems.* New York: Appleton, 1967.

Glasser, W. *Schools without failure.* New York: Harper & Row, 1969.

Goldstein, A., & Dean, S. *The investigation of psychotherapy: Commentaries and readings.* New York: Wiley, 1966.

Gordon, W. M., & Berlyne, D. B. Drive-level and flexibility in paired-associate nonsense syllable learning. *Quarterly Journal of Experimental Psychology*, 1954, **6**, 181–185.

Gotts, E. E., Adams, R. A., & Phillips, B. N. Personality classification of discrete pupil behaviors. *Journal of School Psychology,* 1968–1969, **7,** (3), 54–62.

Gotts, E. E., & Phillips, B. N. The relation between psychometric measures of anxiety and masculinity-femininity. *Journal of School Psychology,* 1968, **6,** 123–129.

Grinker, R. R., Sr. The psychosomatic aspects of anxiety. In C. D. Spielberger (Ed.), *Anxiety and behavior.* New York: Academic Press, 1966.

Guilford, J. P. *Fundamental statistics in psychology and education.* New York: McGraw-Hill, 1965.

Hall, C. S., & Lindzey, G. *Theories of personality.* New York: Wiley, 1957.

Harrison, R. Cognitive change and participation in a sensitivity-training laboratory. *Journal of Consulting Psychology,* 1966, **30,** 517–520.

Hawkes, T., & Koff, R. *Social class differences in anxiety of elementary school children.* Paper presented at the annual meeting of the American Educational Research Association, Los Angeles, February 1969.

Hill, K. Relation of test anxiety, defensiveness, and intelligence to sociometric status. *Child Development,* 1963, **34,** 767–776.

Hill, K., & Sarason, S. B. A further longitudinal study of the relation of test anxiety and defensiveness to test and school performance over the elementary school years. *Child Development Monographs,* 1966, **31,** 1–76.

Hollister, W. G. The concept of strens in preventive interventions and ego-strength building in the schools. In N. Lambert (Ed.), *The protection and promotion of mental health in schools.* (Mental Health Monograph No. 5) Washington, D.C.: United States Government Printing Office, 1965.

Horn, J. An empirical comparison of methods for estimating factor scores. *Educational and Psychological Measurement,* 1965, **25,** 313–322.

Hunter, C. *Classroom climate and pupil characteristics in special classes for the educationally handicapped.* Paper presented at the annual meeting of the American Psychological Association, San Francisco, August 1968.

Iscoe, I., Pierce-Jones, J., Friedman, S. T., & McGhearty, L. Some strategies in mental health consultation: A brief description of a project and some preliminary results. In E. Cowen, E. Gardner, & M. Zax (Eds.), *Emergent approaches to mental health problems.* New York: Appleton, 1967.

Izard, C. E. Anxiety: A variable combination of interacting fundamental emotions. In C. D. Spielberger (Ed.), *Anxiety: Current trends in theory and research.* Vol. 1. New York: Academic Press, 1972.

Izard, C. E., & Tomkins, S. S. Affect and behavior: Anxiety as a negative affect. In C. D. Spielberger (Ed.), *Anxiety and behavior.* New York: Academic Press, 1966.

Jackson, P. W. *Life in classrooms.* New York: Holt, Rinehart & Winston, 1968.

Johnson, S. M. Self-reinforcement vs. external reinforcement in behavior modification with children. *Developmental Psychology,* 1970, **3,** 147–148.

Johnston, J. M., & Johnston, G. T. Modification of consonant speech-sound articulation in young children. *Journal of Applied Behavior Analysis,* 1972, **5,** 233–246.

Kagan, J. Acquisition and significance of sex typing and sex role identity. In M. L. Hoffman & L. W. Hoffman (Eds.), *Review of child development research.* Vol. 1. New York: Russell Sage Foundation, 1964.

Kagan, J., & Moss, H. A. *Birth to maturity: A study in psychological development.* New York: Wiley, 1962.

Katz, I. Academic motivation and equal educational opportunity. *Harvard Educational Review,* 1968, **38,** 57–65.

Kissell, S. Stress-reducing properties of social stimuli. *Journal of Personality and Social Psychology,* 1965, **2,** 378–384.

Klein, D. C., & Lindemann, E. Preventive intervention in individual and family crisis situations. In G. Caplan (Ed.), *Prevention of mental disorders in children.* New York: Basic Books, 1961.

Klein, E. Psychoanalytic aspects of school problems. In A. Freud, H. Hartman & E. Kris (Eds.), *Psychoanalytic study of the child,* New York: International Universities Press, Inc., 1949.

Kohn, M. Social class and the exercise of parental authority. *American Sociological Review,* 1959, **24,** 352–366.

Kohn, M., & Carroll, E. Social class and the allocation of parental responsibilities. *Sociometry,* 1960, **23,** 372–392.

Koval, C., & Hales, L. The effects of the DUSO guidance program on self-concepts of primary school children. *Child Study Journal,* 1972, **2,** 57–61.

Lazarus, R. S. *Psychological stress and the coping process.* New York: McGraw-Hill, 1966.

Lazarus, R. S., & Opton, E. M. The study of psychological stress: A summary of theoretical formulations and experimental findings. In C. D. Spielberger (Ed.), *Anxiety and behavior.* New York: Academic Press, 1966.

Leary, T., & Coffey, H. S. Interpersonal diagnosis: Some problems of methodology and validation. *Journal of Abnormal and Social Psychology,* 1955, **50,** 110–124.

LeKarczyk, D. T., & Hill, K. T. Self-esteem, test anxiety, stress, and verbal learning. *Developmental Psychology,* 1969, **1,** 147–154.

Lewis, W. W. Project Re-Ed: Educational intervention in discordant child rearing systems. In E. Cowen, E. Gardner, & M. Zax (Eds.), *Emergent approaches to mental health problems.* New York: Appleton, 1967.

Lighthall, F. Defensive and non-defensive changes in children's responses to personality questionnaires. *Child Development,* 1963, **34,** 455–470.

Lovitt, T. C., & Curtis, K. A. Academic response rate as a function of teacher- and self-imposed contingencies. *Journal of Applied Behavior Analysis,* 1969, **2,** 49–53.

Maas, H. Some special class differences in the family systems and group relations of pre- and early adolescents. *Child Development,* 1951, **22,** 145–152.

Maccoby, E. E. (Ed.) *The development of sex differences.* Palo Alto, Calif.: Stanford University Press, 1966.

Maccoby, E. E., & Jacklin, C. N. *The psychology of sex differences.* Palo Alto, Calif.: Stanford University Press, 1975.

Malmo, R. B. Studies of anxiety: Some clinical origins of the activation concept. In C. D. Spielberger (Ed.), *Anxiety and behavior.* New York: Academic Press, 1966.

Mandler, G., & Watson, D. L. Anxiety and the interruption of behavior. In C. D. Spielberger (Ed.), *Anxiety and behavior.* New York: Academic Press, 1966.

Marlett, N. J., & Watson, D. Test anxiety and immediate or delayed feedback in a test-like avoidance task. *Journal of Personality and Social Psychology,* 1968, **8,** 200–203.

McNeil, K. A., & Phillips, B. N. Scholastic nature of responses to the environment in selected subcultures. *Journal of Educational Psychology,* 1969, **60,** 79–85.

Mehus, H. Learning and therapy. *American Journal of Orthopsychiatry,* 1953, **23,** 416–421.

Meichenbaum, D. Examination of model characteristics in reducing avoidance behavior. *Journal of Personality and Social Psychology,* 1971, **17,** 298–307.

Meichenbaum, D., & Goodman, J. Reflection-impulsivity and verbal control of motor behavior. *Child Development,* 1969, **40,** 785–797.

Meichenbaum, D., Turk, D., & Burstein, S. The nature of coping with stress. In I. G. Sarason & C. D. Spielberger (Eds.), *Stress and anxiety.* Vol. 2. New York: Wiley, 1975.

Miles, M. B. (Ed.) *Innovation in education.* New York: Teachers College, Columbia University, 1964.

Miller, D. R., & Swanson, G. R. *Inner conflict and defense.* New York: Holt, Rinehart, & Winston, 1960.

Miron, M. S., & Osgood, C. E. Language behavior: The multivariate structure of qualification. In R. Cattell (Ed.), *Handbook of multivariate experimental psychology*. Chicago: Rand McNally, 1966.

Morse, W. C., Cutler, R. L., & Fink, A. H. *Public school classes for the emotionally handicapped: A research analysis*. Washington, D.C.: National Education Association, 1964.

Muus, R. E. A comparison of "high causally" and "low causally" oriented sixth grade children in respect to a perceptual "intolerance of ambiguity" test. *Child Development*, 1960, **31**, 521–536.

Newman, R. G. *Psychological consultation in the schools*. New York: Basic Books, 1967.

Ng, S. N. School anxiety and achievement of children in a Malaysian primary school: A preliminary study. *Jurnal Pedidikan (The Journal of Educational Research)*, 1971, **2**, 41–53.

Nicholson, W. M. The influence of anxiety upon learning: Interference or drive increment? *Journal of Personality*, 1958, **26**, 303–319.

Nijhawan, H. K. *Anxiety in school children*. New Delhi, India: Wiley Eastern Private Ltd., 1972.

Ojemann, R. H. Investigations on the effects of teaching on understanding and appreciation of behavioral dynamics. In G. Caplan (Ed.), *Prevention of mental disorders in children*. New York: Basic Books, 1961.

Ojemann, R. H. Incorporating psychological concepts in the school curriculum. In H. F. Clarizio (Ed.), *Mental health and the educative processes*. Chicago: Rand McNally, 1969.

Ojemann, R. H., & Snider, B. C. The effect of a teaching program in behavioral sciences on changes in causal behavior scores. *Journal of Experimental Education*, 1964, **57**, 255–257.

O'Neil, H. F., Spielberger, C. D., & Hansen, D. N. Effects of state anxiety and task difficulty on computer-assisted learning. *Journal of Educational Psychology*, 1969, **60**, 343–350.

Paivio, A., Baldwin, A., & Berger, A. A measurement of children's sensitivity to audiences. *Child Development*, 1961, **32**, 721–730.

Pannu, P. S. *A conceptual and empirical analysis of anxiety-inducing elementary school situations*. Unpublished doctoral dissertation, University of Texas, Austin, 1974.

Pearson, G. H. A survey of learning difficulties in children. In R. S. Eissler et al. (Eds.), *The psychoanalytic study of the child*, New York: International Universities Press, Inc. 1952.

Phillips, B. N. Effect of cohesion and intelligence on the problem solving efficiency of small face to face groups in cooperative and competitive situations. *Journal of Educational Research*, 1956, **26**, 127–132.

Phillips, B. N. Sex, social class, and anxiety as sources of variation in school achievement. *Journal of Educational Psychology*, 1962, **53**, 316–322.

Phillips, B. N. *An analysis of causes of anxiety among children in school.* (Final Rep., Proj. No. 2616, U.S.O.E. Cooperative Research Branch) Austin, Texas: University of Texas, 1966.(a)

Phillips, B. N. Conflict theory and sex differences on the CMAS. *American Educational Research Journal,* 1966, **3**, 19–25.(b)

Phillips, B. N. Defensiveness as a factor in sex differences in anxiety. *Journal of Consulting Psychology,* 1966, **30**, 167–169.(c)

Phillips, B. N. Anxiety as a function of early school experience. *Psychology in the Schools,* 1967, **4**, 335–340.(a)

Phillips, B. N. The teacher-psychological specialist model. *Journal of School Psychology,* 1967, **6**, 67–71.(b)

Phillips, B. N. The diagnosis-intervention class and the teacher-psychological specialist: Models for the school psychological services network. *Psychology in the Schools,* 1968, **5**, 135–139.

Phillips, B. N. School stress as a factor in children's responses to tests and testing. *Journal of Educational Measurement,* 1971, **8**, 21–26.

Phillips, B. N., & DeVault, M. V. Relation of positive and negative sociometric valuations to social and personal adjustment of school children. *Journal of Applied Psychology,* 1955, **39**, 409–412.

Phillips, B. N., & DeVault, M. V. *Psychology.* Austin, Texas: Steck Co., 1959.

Phillips, B. N., Hindsman, E., & Jennings, E. Influence of intelligence on anxiety and perception of self and others. *Child Development,* 1960, **31**, 41–46.

Phillips, B. N., Martin, R. P., & Meyers, J. Interventions in relation to anxiety in school. In C. D. Spielberger (Ed.), *Anxiety: Current trends in theory and research.* Vol. 2. New York: Academic Press, 1972.

Phillips, B. N., Martin, R. P., & Zorman, L. Factorial structure of the Children's School Questionnaire in American and Slovenian samples. *Journal of Cross-Cultural Psychology,* 1971, **2**, 65–76.

Porter, R. B., & Cattell, R. B. *The Children's Personality Questionnaire.* Champaign, Ill.: Institute of Personality & Abilities Testing, 1963.

Prentice, N. M., & Sperry, B. M. Therapeutically oriented tutoring of children with primary neurotic learning inhibitions. *American Journal of Orthopsychiatry,* 1965, **35**, 521–530.

Proger, B., Mann, L., Taylor, R. C., & Morrell, J. *The relationship between frequency of testing, arithmetic achievement, and induced test anxiety in sixth grade students.* Paper presented at the annual meeting of the American Educational Research Association, Los Angeles, February 1969.

Pyper, J. *Motivation and mathemagenic behaviors: Toward a theory of inserting questions in instructional material.* Paper presented at the annual meeting of the American Educational Research Association, Los Angeles, February 1969.

Reiter, H. H. Some personality correlates of the Page Fantasy Scale. *Perceptual and Motor Skills,* 1963, **16,** 747–748.

Resnick, L. B. Applying applied reinforcement. In R. Glasser (Ed.), *The nature of reinforcement.* New York: Academic Press, 1971.

Richardson, F. Anxiety management training: A cognitive and multimodal approach. In A. Lazarus (Ed.), *Multimodal behavior therapy.* New York: Springer, 1976.

Roen, S. R. Primary prevention in the classroom through a teaching program in the behavioral sciences. In E. Cowen, E. Gardner, & M. Zax (Eds.), *Emergent approaches to mental health problems.* New York: Appleton, 1967.

Ross, D. Relationship between dependency, intentional learning, and incidental learning in preschool children. *Journal of Personality and Social Psychology,* 1966, **4,** 374–381.

Rothkopf, E. Z. Learning from written instructive material: An exploration of the control of inspection behavior by test-like events. *American Educational Research Journal,* 1966, **3,** 241–249.

Rothkopf, E. Z. The concept of mathemagenic activities. *Review of Educational Research,* 1970, **40,** 325–336.

Rubel, A. J. *Across the tracks: Mexican Americans in a Texas city.* Austin: University of Texas Press, 1966.

Ruebush, B. K. *Anxiety.* In H. W. Stevenson, J. Kagan, & C. Spiker (Eds.), *Child Psychology.* 62nd N.S.S.E. Yearbook. Chicago: University of Chicago Press, 1963.

Sarason, I. G. Effect of anxiety and two kinds of motivational instruction on serial learning. *Journal of Abnormal and Social Psychology,* 1957, **54,** 166–171.

Sarason, I. G. The effects of anxiety, reassurance, and meaningfulness of material to be learned, on verbal learning. *Journal of Experimental Psychology,* 1958, **56,** 472–477.

Sarason, I. G. Characteristics of three measures of anxiety. *Journal of Clinical Psychology,* 1961, **17,** 196–197.

Sarason, I. G. Test anxiety and intellectual performance. *Journal of Abnormal and Social Psychology,* 1963, **66,** 73–75.

Sarason, I. G. Experimental approaches to test anxiety: Attention and the uses of information. In C. D. Spielberger (Ed.), *Anxiety: Current trends in theory and research.* Vol. 2. New York: Academic Press, 1972.

Sarason, I. G. Anxiety and self-preoccupation. In I. G. Sarason and C.

Spielberger (Eds.), *Stress and anxiety.* Vol. 2. New York: Wiley, 1975.(a)

Sarason, I. G. Test anxiety and the self-disclosing coping model. *Journal of Consulting and Clinical Psychology,* 1975, **43,** 148–153.(b)

Sarason, I. G., & Minard, J. Test anxiety, experimental instructions, and the Wechsler Adult Intelligence Scale. *Journal of Educational Psychology,* 1962, **53,** 299–302.

Sarason, I. G., Pederson, A. M., & Nyman, B. A. Test anxiety and the observation of models. *Journal of Personality,* 1968, **36,** 493–511.

Sarason, S. B. The measurement of anxiety in children: Some questions and problems. In C. D. Spielberger (Ed.), *Anxiety and behavior.* New York: Academic Press, 1966.

Sarason, S. B. *The culture of school and the problems of change.* Boston: Allyn & Bacon, 1971.

Sarason, S. B. Anxiety, intervention and the culture of school. In C. D. Spielberger (Ed.), *Anxiety: Current trends in theory and research.* New York: Academic Press, 1972.

Sarason, S. B., Davidson, K., Lighthall, F., & Waite, R. A test anxiety scale for children. *Child Development,* 1958, **29,** 105–113.

Sarason, S. B., Davidson, K. S., Lighthall, F. F., Waite, R. R., & Ruebush, B. K. *Anxiety in elementary school children.* New York: Wiley, 1960.

Sarason, S. B., Hill, K., & Zimbardo, P. G. A longitudinal study of the relation of test anxiety to performance on intelligence and achievement tests. *Child Development Monographs,* 1964, **29,** 1–51.

Sarason, S. B., Levine, M. Goldenberg, I. I., Cherlin, D. L., & Bennett, E. M. *Psychology in community settings.* New York: Wiley, 1966.

Sarbin, T. R. Ontology recapitulates philology: The mythic nature of anxiety. *American Psychologist,* 1968, **23,** 411–418.

Schachter, S. *The psychology of affiliation.* Palo Alto, Calif.: Stanford University Press, 1959.

Schachter, S. Birth order and sociometric choice. *Journal of Abnormal and Social Psychology,* 1964, **68,** 453–456.

Schilhab, J. E. *Influences of psycho-social factors in a newly integrated school.* Unpublished doctoral dissertation, University of Texas, Austin, 1976.

Schultz, J. P., Firetto, A., & Walker, R. The relationship of parental assessment and anxiety in high school freshmen. *Psychology in the Schools,* 1969, **6,** 311–312.

Selye, H. *The stress of life.* New York: McGraw-Hill, 1956.

Shaw, M. C., & McCuen, J. T. The onset of academic under-achievement in bright children. *Journal of Educational Psychology,* 1960, **51,** 103–108.

Sieber, J. E. A paradigm for experimental modification of the effects of test anxiety on cognitive processes. *American Educational Research Journal,* 1969, **6**, 46–61.

Singer, J. L., & Rowe, R. An experimental study of some relationships between daydreaming and anxiety. *Journal of Consulting Psychology,* 1962, **26**, 446–454.

Singer, J. L., & Schonbar, R. A. Correlates of day-dreaming: A dimension of self-awareness. *Journal of Consulting Psychology,* 1961, **25**, 1–6.

Spence, J. T., & Spence, K. W. The motivational components of manifest anxiety: Drive and drive stimuli. In C. D. Spielberger (Ed.), *Anxiety and behavior.* New York: Academic Press, 1966.

Spielberger, C. D. (Ed.), *Anxiety and behavior.* New York: Academic Press, 1966.

Spielberger, C. D. Theory and research on anxiety. In C. D. Spielberger (Ed.), *Anxiety and behavior.* New York: Academic Press, 1966.

Spielberger, C. D. (Ed.), *Anxiety: Current trends in theory and research.* 2 Vols. New York: Academic Press, 1972.

Spielberger, C. D., & Smith, L. H. Anxiety, stress, and serial-position effects in serial-verbal learning. *Journal of Experimental Psychology,* 1966, **72**, 589–595.

Stanford, D., Dember, W., & Stanford, L. A children's form of the Alpert–Haber achievement anxiety scale. *Child Development,* 1963, **34**, 1027–1032.

Stephens, J. M. *The process of schooling: A psychological examination.* New York: Holt, Rinehart, & Winston, 1967.

Stouffer, G. A., & Owens, J. Behavioral problems of children as identified by today's teachers and compared with those reported by E. K. Wickman. *Journal of Educational Research,* 1955, **40**, 321–331.

Sutton-Smith., B., & Rosenberg, B. G. Manifest anxiety and game preference in children. *Child Development,* 1960, **31**, 307–311.

Taylor, R. G. Personality traits and discrepant achievement: A review. *Journal of Consulting Psychology,* 1964, **11**, 76–81.

Thorndike, R. L. *The concepts of over- and under-achievement.* New York: Columbia University Press, 1963.

Tobias, S., & Williamson, J. *Anxiety and response to programmed instruction.* Paper presented at the annual meeting of the American Educational Research Association, Chicago, February 1968.

Tolor, A., & Lane, P. An experimental approach to the treatment of disturbed school-aged children. *Journal of School Psychology,* 1968, **6**, 97–103.

Tseng, M. S., & Thompson, D. L. *Need achievement, fear of failure, perception of occupational prestige, and occupational aspirations of adolescents of differ-*

ent socio-economic groups. Paper presented at the annual meeting of the American Educational Research Association, Los Angeles, February 1969.

Waite, R. R., Sarason, S. B., Lighthall, F. F., & Davidson, K. S. A study of anxiety and learning in children. *Journal of Abnormal and Social Psychology,* 1958, **57,** 267–270.

Walker, H. M., & Buckley, N. K. Programming generalization and maintenance of treatment effects across time and across settings. *Journal of Applied Behavior Analysis,* 1972, **5,** 209–224.

Walker, R. E. *The interaction between failure, manifest anxiety, and task-irrelevant responses in paired-associate learning.* Unpublished doctoral dissertation, Northwestern University, 1961.

Walters, R. H., & Karal, P. Social deprivation and verbal behavior. *Journal of Personality,* 1960, **28,** 89–107.

Weinstock, A. R. Family environment and the development of defense and coping mechanisms. *Journal of Personality and Social Psychology,* 1967, **5,** 67–75.

Wickman, E. K. *Children's behavior and teacher attitudes.* New York: Commonwealth Fund, 1928.

Wiggins, J. S. Personality structure. In P. R. Farnsworth (Ed.), *Annual review of psychology.* Palo Alto, Calif.: Annual Reviews, Inc., 1968.

Williams, D. H. *A comparison of instructional practices of graded and nongraded classes in an elementary school setting.* Unpublished doctoral dissertation, University of Texas, Austin, 1968.

Williams, E. *Effects of inter-group discussion on social distance and personal space of black and white students.* Unpublished doctoral dissertation, University of Texas, Austin, 1972.

Witkin, H. A., Dyk, R. B., Faterson, H. F., Goodenough, D. R., & Karp, S. A. *Psychological differentiation: Studies of development.* New York: Wiley, 1962.

Wolpe, J. The conditioning and deconditioning of neurotic anxiety. In C. D. Spielberger (Ed.), *Anxiety and behavior.* New York: Academic Press, 1966.

Zimiles, H. Preventive aspects of school experience. In E. Cowen, E. Gardner, & M. Zax (Eds.), *Emergent approaches to mental health problems.* New York: Appleton, 1967.

Zweibelson, I. Test anxiety and intelligence test performance. *Journal of Consulting Psychology,* 1956, **20,** 479–481.

DATE DUE